DIALOGUE WITH DEATH

Novels
The Gladiators
Darkness at Noon
Arrival and Departure
Thieves in the Night
The Age of Longing
The Call Girls

Autobiography
Dialogue with Death
Scum of the Earth
Arrow in the Blue
The Invisible Writing
The God that Failed (with others)
Stranger on the Square (with Cynthia Koestler)

Essays
The Yogi and the Commissar
The Challenge of our Time
Insight and Outlook
Promise and Fulfilment
The Trail of the Dinosaur
Reflections on Hanging
The Sleepwalkers
The Lotus and the Robot
Control of the Mind
The Act of Creation
Suicide of a Nation (edited)
The Ghost in the Machine
Drinkers of Infinity
The Age of Longing
The Case of the Midwife Toad
The Roots of Coincidence
The Lion and the Ostrich
The Heel of Achilles
The Thirteenth Tribe
Astride the Two Cultures
Twentieth Century Views
Janus: A Summing Up
Bricks to Babel

Theater
Twilight Bar

ARTHUR KOESTLER

Dialogue with Death

*The Journal of a Prisoner of the Fascists
in the Spanish Civil War*

Translated by
TREVOR AND PHYLLIS BLEWITT

With a New Introduction by
LOUIS MENAND

The University of Chicago Press

The University of Chicago Press, Chicago 60637
Copyright © 1946 by Arthur Koestler
Preface copyright © 1966 by Arthur Koestler
Introduction copyright © 2011 by Louis Menand
All rights reserved.
University of Chicago Press edition 2011
Printed in the United States of America

20 19 18 17 16 15 14 13 12 11   1 2 3 4 5

ISBN-13: 978-0-226-44961-6 (paper)
ISBN-10: 0-226-44961-0 (paper)

Library of Congress Cataloging-in-Publication Data

Koestler, Arthur, 1905–1983.
Dialogue with death : the journal of a prisoner of the fascists in the Spanish
Civil War/ by Arthur Koestler ; with a new introduction by Louis Menand ;
translated by Trevor and Phyllis Blewitt.
p. cm.
Originally written in German.
ISBN-13: 978-0-226-44961-6 (pbk. : alk. paper)
ISBN-10: 0-226-44961-0 (pbk. : alk. paper) 1. Koestler, Arthur,
1905–1983—Imprisonment. 2. Journalists—Europe—Biography. 3.
Political prisoners—Spain—Biography. 4. Spain—History—Civil War,
1936–1939—Prisoners and prisons. 5. Spain—History—Civil War,
1936–1939—Personal narratives. I. Menand, Louis. II. Blewitt, Phyllis. III.
Blewitt, Trevor, 1900– IV. Title.
DP269.9.K613 2011
[PR6021.04Z46]
946.081′1—DC22

2010041525

ARTHUR KOESTLER was thirty-one when he was arrested by Francisco Franco's Nationalist forces in Málaga, Spain—the event that led to the experiences he recounts in *Dialogue with Death*. Koestler was visiting Spain, in the midst of the Civil War, as a correspondent for a British paper called the *News Chronicle*. Why he chose to remain in Málaga after the city had been abandoned by Republican troops and most of its inhabitants is unclear even in his own telling. He may have felt loyal to the acting British consul, Sir Peter Chalmers Mitchell, with whom he had become friendly; he may have wanted to demonstrate his bravery in a situation where others had not; he may have hoped to get a big scoop. These motives—loyalty, courage, and ambition—are all plausible, because they are all characteristic of the man.

Koestler was the prototype of the rootless cosmopolite. History made him that way. He was born in Budapest in 1905. His family fled when the short-lived Communist government fell, in 1919, amid the ensuing White Terror. They moved to Vienna (Koestler's mother was Austrian), where Koestler attended the Technische Hochschule. He was not a successful student, and, in 1925, after his father's business collapsed, he was expelled for nonpayment of fees. He moved to Palestine—the family was Jewish, and Koestler had been involved in Zionist organizations in Vienna—and began a career as a journalist.

After several years of reporting from the Middle East, Koestler left, abruptly, for Berlin, arriving on September 14, 1930, the same day that the National Socialist Party made its great gains in the Reichstag elections. He became the science editor on a major newspaper there, but was let go, for reasons that are uncertain, in 1932. The following year, he traveled through the Soviet Union, working on a book and visiting many of the republics, including Turkmenistan, in central Asia. By the time that trip ended, it was not safe for Koestler to return to Germany, so he moved to Paris, and soon after married his first wife, Dorothee. He was living in Paris when he embarked on his Spanish adventure.

Koestler's imprisonment became an international cause. William Randolph Hearst called his arrest an "unacceptable infringement of the rights of journalists to carry out their profession." The French government was urged to intervene, and Koestler's wife enlisted British notables in the cause. The National Association of Journalists, in Britain, sent a resolution to the British government demanding it to intercede, and fifty-six members of Parliament signed a letter in Koestler's support.

Finally, following negotiations involving the League of Nations, the Red Cross, and the Vatican, a prisoner exchange was arranged, and Koestler returned to England to find himself a famous man. A crowd of reporters met him as he walked off the boat. Three and a half years later, he published *Darkness at Noon*, his classic novel about a man confined, interrogated, and executed in a Communist prison. Though the book did not do well in England, it was an enormous bestseller in the United States and, after the end of the Second World War, in France and around the world. The novel brought Koestler financial security for the rest of his life; it has never gone out of print.

Koestler went on to produce several volumes of autobiography—*The Scum of the Earth* (1941), *Arrow in the Blue* (1952), and *The Invisible Writing* (1954). All were popular successes.

He produced other novels, as well, including *The Gladiators* (1939), based on Spartacus's slave revolt; *Arrival and Departure* (1943), about a young revolutionary who escapes from a Nazi prison; and *Thieves in the Night* (1946), a story set in Palestine. Those books had a more uneven reception. After the war, Koestler became intensively involved with anti-Communist organizations, notably the Congress for Cultural Freedom. But in 1952, apparently having realized that his anti-Communism was too hard-line for his liberal colleagues, he more or less retired from politics and began writing popular books on science, among them *The Sleepwalkers* (1959), *The Lotus and the Robot* (1961), *The Ghost in the Machine* (1967), and *The Case of the Midwife Toad* (1971).

Koestler's life was a geopolitical adventure story—assiduously and admirably sorted out by Michael Scammell in his biography *Koestler: The Literary and Political Odyssey of a Twentieth-Century Skeptic* (2009). He was a person who, in the course of his career, managed to attract the wrong kind of interest from the Gestapo, the Sûreté, MI5, and, almost certainly, the NKVD. (His relations with the CIA were friendly.) He was imprisoned in three countries. He lived, at various points in his life, in England, Wales, and France—once in a villa he bought on the banks of the Seine across from the forest of Fontainebleau. He also spent several years in the United States, in a farmhouse in Bucks County, in Pennsylvania. And he traveled, in search of esoteric wisdom, to India and Japan.

He maintained lifelong relationships (interrupted by the occasional feud) with the writers, scientists, and political activists he met in the various places he traveled. And he was a social and sexual torpedo. Academics generally condescended to or avoided him, but he socialized and debated—alcohol, a necessary lubricant, made him almost always obstreperous and occasionally violent—with nearly everyone else in midcentury intellectual circles, from George Orwell and Jean-Paul Sartre to Whittaker Chambers and Timothy Leary. He married three times and had, literally, hundreds of affairs.

In 1983, afflicted with Parkinson's disease and chronic lymphatic leukemia, he committed suicide by taking an overdose of alcohol and barbiturates. His third wife, Cynthia, killed herself alongside him; she was fifty-five and in good health. Koestler had by then become infatuated with the fringes of scientific research—with theories about things like levitation, extrasensory perception, and the heritability of acquired characteristics. He left virtually his entire estate, four hundred thousand pounds, to fund an academic chair in parapsychology, and there is today a Koestler Parapsychology Unit in the Department of Psychology at the University of Edinburgh.

Dialogue with Death was composed in German (as was *Darkness at Noon*) and translated prior to publication. It first appeared in Great Britain in 1937, as part of a volume called *Spanish Testament*. In 1942, Koestler revised it and brought it out as a separate book. The experiences he describes in it are one source for the fictional Stalinist prison in *Darkness at Noon*—though the novel also incorporates details reported by an old Budapest friend, Eva Striker, who had emigrated to the Soviet Union and was arrested there in 1936, at the height of the purges, and charged with plotting to assassinate Stalin. (She was released after her interrogator was himself arrested.)

There is no reason to doubt anything in the account Koestler gives in *Dialogue with Death* of his arrest and his ninety-four days in captivity, but there is one major elision. As he made clear in the preface he wrote for the 1967 reprinting of the book, contrary to what William Randolph Hearst, the fifty-six MPs, and the League of Nations may have believed, Koestler was not really a journalist when he went to Spain. He was exactly what Franco suspected him of being: a Communist agent. And so he genuinely was, for those three months, at every moment on the verge of being shot. Oddly, this elision (or evasion) is what gives this nonfiction book a kind of literary permanence that *Darkness at Noon* lacks. If it included details about Koestler's assignment in Spain, it would be a fascinating but dated text—a document, rather than the expression of something about the human condition.

Koestler had become a Communist in Berlin in 1931. He remained undercover in order not to compromise his position at the paper, where it was felt he could be of most use to the Party. His own narrative of this part of his life appears in what is, after *Darkness at Noon*, the most widely read thing he wrote, the apologia for his Communist past in the anthology *The God that Failed* (1949), edited by his friend the British MP Richard Crossman. Koestler's own interpretation of his dismissal from the Berlin paper was that he was betrayed by a source he had recruited, the son of a high-ranking German diplomat, who had become panicked by his role in passing information to a foreign power—that is, to the Soviet Union. It was therefore not because he was a Jew that Koestler did not return to Berlin at the end of 1933. It was because he was a Communist. The Reichstag fire in February 1933, blamed on Communist agents, led to a suspension of civil liberties— Hitler had come to power in January—and a crackdown on suspected Communists.

When he reached Paris, Koestler was enrolled in the apparat of the formidable Stalinist agent Willi Münzenberg, also a German exile. It was Münzenberg's idea to send Koestler to Spain: his mission was to find evidence, to be used by the Party, of German and Italian support for Franco's insurgency. And it was Münzenberg who arranged, through an editor at the *News Chronicle*, also a Party member, for Koestler's press credentials, to be used as a cover. So when Dorothee campaigned for her husband's release, she had to conceal his Party affiliation—and, at the same time, to fight against the Party's own preference, which was that Koestler be kept in prison as long as possible, or even executed by Franco, as a martyr to the anti-Fascist cause.

Dialogue with Death's remarkable currency is owed to the fact that, unlike *Darkness at Noon*, it is not really about politics. Koestler did not think much of the Fascists, but he saw little to admire in the Republicans, either. His book is simply about what it is like to face one's imminent execution. It was admired by Sartre as a lucid statement of the existentialist situation—and, in this respect, it is a stranger and stronger book than *Darkness at Noon*. *Darkness at Noon* is a *roman à thèse*: every character is a type—the disillusioned old revolutionary, the callow young revolutionary, the soulless apparatchik, the doomed idealist. *Dialogue with Death* is a simple report on a series of mostly horrible events, and the author is under no obligation to organize them, or even to make sense of them.

As a consequence, the accidents and absurdity of life are represented simply as they were experienced—although, since it is a life under immense pressure, the incidents are often tragic or grotesque. There is Carlos, the Italian army officer who, feeling he had been compelled to suffer some indignity or other, punches a Spanish police officer in the nose and ends up in a cell block of condemned men. There is the orderly Manuel, rumored to have been sentenced to life for "some sexual offense that had a fatal outcome," and his late-night game of horse with the sadistic warder Koestler calls "Captain Bligh." And there is the night during Koestler's stay in the Málaga slaughterhouse when he wakes up and hears a prisoner singing "The Internationale"—an act the prisoner must know will guarantee his execution.

"We were never more free than during the German occupation," Sartre famously wrote in 1944. The remark is a little self-dramatizing, also possibly a little unearned. Sartre was, briefly, following the German invasion of France, a prisoner of war, but he was not in serious danger, and for most of the occupation he led a relatively cautious and secure life. One doesn't feel this way about the words that Koestler published in *Dialogue with Death*, two years earlier: "Often when I wake at night I am homesick for my cell in the death-house in Seville and, strangely enough, I feel that I have never been so *free* as I was then." When he and the other prisoners knew that they were going to die but no longer feared dying, he writes, "at such moments we were free—men without shadows, dismissed from the ranks of the mortal; it was the most complete experience of freedom that can be granted a man."

It is interesting that even in 1942, when he published the revised edition of *Dialogue with Death*, Koestler did not reveal his Communist associations. He had long before resigned from the Party, in 1938, and he was profoundly affected by the signing of the nonagression pact between Hitler and Stalin in August 1939—the treaty that made possible Hitler's invasion of Poland. "Our feelings towards Russia were rather like that of a man who has divorced a much-beloved wife," he wrote in his autobiographical account of those years, *Scum of the Earth*. "He hates her and yet it is a sort of consolation for him to know that she is still there, on the same planet, still young and alive. Now she was dead." The friend of his enemy had become his enemy.

It is not likely that Koestler was embarrassed about his Communist past. He would write openly about it just a few years later, in *The God that Failed*; and, in any case, he seems a man who was embarrassed by nothing. He must have seen that the reasons for finding himself in the situation he describes in *Dialogue with Death* are not important. Between 1933 and 1945, millions of Europeans, the grand and the ordinary, the infamous and the insignificant, found themselves confronted with the knock on the door, with an imminent threat of annihilation. *Dialogue with Death* is the story of a man who escaped, and only by a hair, his own knock on the door. Koestler thought that the lesson he learned in Spain was not about Fascism or Communism, but about the irreducibility of individual life. For death is the one experience that cannot be mediated—either by other people, or by a theory of history.

Each person faces his or her extinction alone. It is, as Koestler puts it, a dialogue with just two speakers.

Koestler regretted, he said in *The God that Failed*, that the conclusions he drew from his Spanish imprisonment could be expressed only in "the dowdy guise of perennial commonplaces: that man is a reality, mankind an abstraction; that men cannot be treated as units in operations of political arithmetic because they behave like the symbols for zero and the infinite, which dislocate all mathematical operations; that the end justifies the means only within very narrow limits; that ethics is not a function of social utility, and charity not a petty-bourgeois sentiment but the gravitational force which keeps civilization in its orbit." He had, in his hands, a story for which a straightforward factual presentation was all that was required. It was his genius as a writer not to complicate it.

Louis Menand

In 1937, while working for the London *News Chronicle* as a correspondent with the loyalist forces in the Spanish Civil War, I was captured by General Franco's troops and held for several months in solitary confinement, witnessing the executions of my fellow-prisoners and awaiting my own. *Dialogue with Death* is an account of that experience written immediately after my release, in July-August, 1937, and published at the end of the same year as part of a larger book under the title *Spanish Testament*.

At the time the Civil War was still on, and its outcome still in the balance. This circumstance made it necessary to pass over in silence certain aspects of my adventure which in the public eye would have been damaging to the loyalist cause. I thus felt obliged to conceal three essential facts: that I was a member of the Communist party; that my previous visit to General Franco's headquarters had been undertaken on behalf of the Comintern, using the *News Chronicle* as a cover; and finally, that at the time when I was captured, I was also working for the loyalist Government's official news agency. I have since told this political background story in *The Invisible Writing*. My principal interest in writing *Dialogue with Death* was an introspective one: the psychological impact of the condemned cell. From this point of view, the political background was irrelevant, and the narrative, as far as it went, was the truthful account of an intimate experience.

Nevertheless, the book is indirectly affected by what it conceals, for if the victim was really as innocent as he appears in the text—the *bona fide* correspondent of a respectable English Liberal newspaper—his fear of torture, and his preoccupation with suicide to escape it, must appear unjustified. The reader must find it equally puzzling, in the earlier chapters, that a foreign journalist should take the liberty of accusing a local military commander with 'criminal negligence' and generally behave in a rather authoritative manner. The answer is, that under the chaotic circumstances my Comintern papers, and my connexion with the Government's information department, did carry a certain weight with local commanders. And, once captured by the enemy, I had reason to fear not only General Franco's Intelligence Department, but also the German Gestapo, which intimately collaborated with the former, and which had a long record of my previous activities in Germany, France and Spain.

As often happens in such situations, I did not know (and still do not know) how much my captors knew. The military examiner who interrogated me seemed to know very little; but he may have been biding his time. In the muddle of a civil war dossiers travel slowly, and at the time when my interrogation began the negotiations about my exchange against a hostage in the loyalists' hands had been almost concluded.

Another rather puzzling circumstance is that my examination seems to have begun after sentence had been passed. While I was in prison, General Franco's information department made various vague and contradictory statements on this point. The only authentic information that I was able to obtain later on is the account published by Dr. Marcel Junod, delegate of the International Committee of the Red Cross, who negotiated my exchange, and who was officially informed that I had been sentenced to death.

Dialogue with Death was written in German, except for the prison diary, which I wrote in English to avoid calling the Gestapo's attention to me.

All my books prior to 1940 were written in German, after that date in English.

A. K.

London, 1966

FOREWORD

NONE of the characters in this book is fictitious; most of them are dead by now.

To die—even in the service of an impersonal cause—is always a personal and intimate affair. Thus it was inevitable that these pages, written for the most part in the actual expectancy and fear of death, should bear a private character. There are, in the author's opinion, two reasons which justify their publication.

In the first place, the things which go on inside a condemned man's head have a certain psychological interest. Professional writers have rarely had an opportunity of studying these processes in the first person singular. I have tried to present them as frankly and concisely as I could. The main difficulty was the temptation to cut a good figure; I hope that the reader will agree that I have succeeded in overcoming this.

In the second place, I believe that wars, in particular civil wars, consist of only ten per cent action and of ninety per cent passive suffering. Thus this account of the hermetically sealed Andalusian mortuaries may perhaps bring closer to the reader the nature of Civil War than descriptions of battles.

I dedicate it to my friend Nicolás, an obscure little soldier of the Spanish Republic, who on April 14th, 1937, on the sixth birthday of that Republic, was shot dead in the prison of Seville.

A. K.

DIALOGUE WITH DEATH

"Une vie ne vaut rien—
mais rien ne vaut une vie . . ."
(André Malraux; *Les Conquérants*)

I

FOR the last six weeks there had been a lull in the fighting. The winter was cold; the wind from the Guadarrama whipped Madrid; the Moors in their trenches caught pneumonia and spat blood. The passes in the Sierra Nevada were blocked, the Republican Militiamen had neither uniforms nor blankets and their hospitals had no chloroform; their frozen fingers and feet had to be amputated without their being put to sleep. At the Anarchist hospital in Malaga a boy sang the Marseillaise while they sawed away two of his toes; this expedient gained a certain popularity.

Then spring came and all was well again; the buds on the trees opened and the tanks started on the roads. Nature's benevolence enabled General Queipo de Llano to launch, as early as mid-January, his long-planned offensive against Malaga.

This was in nineteen hundred and thirty-seven. General Gonzales Queipo de Llano, who not so long ago had conspired against the Monarchy and proclaimed his sympathy with communism to all and sundry in the cafés round the Puerta del Sol, was now in command of the Second Division of the insurgent army. He had a microphone installed in a room at his G.H.Q. in Seville and talked into it every night for an hour. "The Marxists," he said, "are ravening beasts, but we are gentlemen. Señor Companys deserves to be stuck like a pig."

General Queipo's army consisted of approximately 50,000 Italian troops, three *banderas* of the Foreign Legion and 15,000 African tribesmen. The rest of his men, about ten per cent, were of Spanish nationality.

The offensive began on January 10th.

I was in Paris at the time. I had written a pamphlet on the Spanish War; the French edition was just out. In the preceding months I had worked as a special correspondent for the *News Chronicle*, first with the insurgents and later, after Franco's propaganda department had kicked me out of Nationalist territory, in Catalonia and Madrid. Now the war had shifted to the Andalusian front and it was decided that I should go there.

I left Paris on January 15th, took train to Toulouse and from there flew to Barcelona. I stayed in Barcelona for only one day. The city presented a depressing picture. There was no bread, no milk, no meat to be had, and there were long queues outside the shops. The Anarchists blamed the Catalan Government for the food shortage and organized an intensive campaign of political agitation; the windows of the trams were plastered with their leaflets. The tension in the city was near danger-point. It looked as though Spain were not only to be the stage for the dress-rehearsal of the second world war, but also for the fratricidal struggle within the European Left.

I was glad not to have to write an article on Barcelona. On the 16th I left by the 4 p.m. train for Valencia with Willy Forrest, also of the *News Chronicle*. His destination was Madrid, mine Malaga.

The train to Valencia was crowded out. Every compartment contained four times as many Militiamen, sitting, lying down or standing, as it was meant to hold. A kindly railway official installed us in a first class carriage and locked the door from the outside so that we should not be disturbed. Scarcely had the train started when four Anarchist Militiamen in the corridor began to hammer at the glass door of our compartment. We tried to open it, but could not; we were trapped in our cage. The guard who had the key had completely vanished. We were unable to make ourselves understood through the locked door owing to the noise of the train, and the Militiamen thought that it was out of sheer ill-will that we were not opening it. Forrest and I could not help grinning, which further enraged the Militiamen, and the situation became more dramatic from minute to minute. Half the coach collected outside the glass door to gaze at the two obviously Fascist agents. At length the guard came and unlocked the door and explained the situation, and then ensued a perfect orgy of fraternizing and eating, and a dreadful hullabaloo of pushing and shouting and singing.

By dawn the train was six hours behind time. It was going so slowly that the Militiamen jumped from the footboards, picked handfuls of oranges from the trees that grew on the edge of the embankment and clambered back again into the carriage amidst general applause. This form of amusement continued until about midday. There was no loss of life; only one man sprained his ankle as he jumped, and stayed sitting on the embankment, evidently *hors-de-combat* so far as the Civil War was concerned.

Valencia too disported itself in the brilliant January sunshine with one weeping and one smiling eye. There was a shortage of paper; some of the newspapers were cut down to four pages, three full of the Civil War, the fourth of football championships, bullfights, theatre and film notices. Two days before our arrival a decree had been issued ordering the famous Valencia cabarets to close at nine o'clock in the evening "in view of the gravity of the situation." Of course they all continued to keep open until one o'clock in the morning, with one exception, and that one adhered strictly to the letter of the law. The owner was later unmasked as a rebel supporter and his cabaret was closed down.

One had often to wait for five to six hours to get through by telephone to London. Some evenings, when I got tired of waiting, I would pop over to the cabaret across the road. There in the boxes the—more or less—pretty cabaret artists sat demurely with their mothers, aunts, brothers and sisters. When their turn came they danced or sang in a state of— more or less—nudity, displaying a greater or lesser degree of talent, then went back to join their mothers and aunts in the boxes and drink lemonade. Had a mere man ventured in their neighbourhood I verily believe he would have been immediately arrested as a Fascist. On the walls hung notices: "Citizens, conduct yourselves with restraint at this grave moment. We grudge no one his amusement, but let there be no frivolity, etc."

In October, when I had last been in Valencia, every second turn had been a nude dance. Now *brassières* and *caches sexe* were *de rigueur*.

Telephoning, by the way, was not without its charms. When one put through a call one had to send a copy of the message one was going to dictate over the phone to the censor, and while one was telephoning the message from one's hotel the censor would be sitting in his office, the text of the message in front of him, listening in. The censorship was strict, but the censors themselves were quite amiable fellows, all of whom one knew personally. If one deviated by a hair's breadth from the text, they would roar into the telephone: "Hi, Arturo, that's not in the manuscript!" "What—what?" the despairing stenographers in London would yell. "That's nothing to do with you," the censor would say. "I'm speaking to Arturo."

On Sunday the 24th a big bullfight was billed to take place in the Plaza del Toro—"in honour of the Russian Ambassador, who has consented to attend in person," announced the newspapers. The proceeds were to be presented to Russia for the construction of a new "Komsomol"; "Komsomol" was the name of a Russian cargo steamer which had been sunk by a rebel ship while bringing provisions for Valencia. But on the Sunday it rained, and it was announced on the wireless, between news bulletins from the front, that the bullfight had unfortunately to be called off.

For days before this, however, the weather was glorious, and a German *émigré* writer took us for a drive along the shore in his car. There were four of us: the German writer, the driver, Forrest and myself. The writer—let us call him Alberto (we all had o's tacked on to our names free and gratis) —was a Political Commissar with the Nth Company of the International Brigade. He was in Valencia on leave from the front. Before the war he had written psychoanalytical novels; nevertheless he looked quite well in uniform. We sprawled on the beach, blinked up at the sun, agreed that with the blue sea before us and the blue sky above us war seemed a highly illogical business, and indulged in similar high-falutin' reflections. When we got back to the car, we found four strange men sitting in it and sweating away trying to start it up, while the driver, a little fourteen-year-old Spanish lad, stood by blubbering, the tears literally pouring down his cheeks.

One of the men asked Alberto for the starting key and remarked that the car had been requisitioned. He produced his authority from some Control Commission or other of the F.A.I. *(Federacion Anarquista Ibérica)*, a paper headed "Down with the misuse of State cars for private pleasure." His three colleagues were also Anarchists. They all had enormous great revolvers such as one only saw in silent Wild West films before the War. I had a suspicion that they loaded them with gunpowder and leaden bullets.

Alberto too produced his identity papers, with a photograph of himself as Political Commissar of the Nth Company, and protested against the requisitioning of his car. By now a crowd had collected—men, women and children either in bathing dresses or uniforms—and was following the scene with friendly interest.

The Anarchist said that he did not think much of a Commissar who, despite the Civil War and the shortage of petrol, used his car for joy-rides along the beach, and the car would be requisitioned.

Alberto said that a soldier needed a little recreation when on leave, and would the Anarchists kindly get out of his car, or he would put them out by force.

The driver, frightened out of his wits, stood there, trying to sniff back up his nose the tears that were running down his cheeks.

The Anarchist chieftain had been trying in the meantime to start the car. From somewhere in the bowels of the maltreated engine there came a groan. This noise threw Alberto into a sudden rage. In an access of poetic fury he seized the Anarchist violently by the sleeve, and roared in German at the top of his voice: *"Raus! Raus!! Raus!!!"*

This greatly impressed the Anarchists. Alberto's rage was obviously a proof of his clear conscience and his *bona fides*. They grinned and scrambled out of the car. "Next time we'll shoot you, all the same," said one of them, giving Alberto a friendly pat on the back with his revolver.

We got in; the driver blew his nose and started up the car, and we drove back to Valencia amid the enthusiastic cheers of the spectators.

On the day before I left for Malaga I attended a parade of troops at Castellon, a seaside town not far from Valencia, at the invitation of General Julio.

General Julio had formerly been Julius Deutsch and Minister of War in the Austrian Republic after the collapse of 1918. His aide-de-camp was a certain Count Reventlow, nephew of the Nazi member of the Reichstag; himself, like Deutsch, a member of the Social-Democratic Party. When the Republic was set up in Austria in 1918 and Julius Deutsch was appointed Minister of War, his first act was to dismiss all the reactionary officers of the old army—exactly what the Spanish Republic in 1931 failed to do. Deutsch was one of the very few men of the Left in Europe who knew anything about strategy and military matters. At that time this was looked upon as bad form in Left-wing circles.

Deutsch was an exception. When the situation in Austria became threatening, he organized the Austrian workers' defence corps, the famous *Schutzbund*. The *Schutzbund* was destroyed in February, 1934, by Dollfuss; but Deutsch was and continued to be the most popular figure of the Austrian Left, loved and respected by the rank and file as scarcely any Socialist leader of the post-war era has ever been.

According to European standards the parade was a wretched, almost comic affair; according to Spanish ideas it was a miracle of discipline and smartness. Drill was carried out with sticks; for the division had only 140 guns amongst 900 men. A company of machine-gunners dismantled and then assembled a machine-gun. General Deutsch pulled out his stop-watch: the exercise had taken ninety seconds—very bad indeed. The company commander stared at him as though he had taken leave of his senses. "What are you staring like that for?" asked General Julio. "I had no idea you timed this sort of thing with a watch," said the company commander, "I thought that was only done at sporting events, but it's a jolly good idea." "I'll buy you a stop-watch," said the General. "That's fine," said the company commander. "The Fascists won't half open their eyes."

They were all full of enthusiasm for *nuestro General*, who wore white cotton gloves, could not speak a word of Spanish and had the most marvellous and rather crazy brainwaves that no one else ever had. He had, for example, invented a kind of

buckle for fastening your spade to your rucksack. Had anyone
ever heard the like of it? It was just like being in a real army.
Nothing was more flattering to these improvised troops of the
Spanish Republic than to be told that they were almost like a
real army.

I was told a great number of anecdotes of the first days of
the Civil War. The men of the famous "Durutti Column," for
instance, had refused to take spades with them to the front,
declaring, with the twofold pride of Catalans and Anarchists:
"We are going to the front to fight and to die, but not to
work." And the first troop of the "Durutti Column" only
realized after a twenty-four hours' journey by rail to the Ara-
gon front that they had forgotten to bring provisions and
cooking equipment; or rather, it had never entered their heads
that a war calls for special feeding arrangements.

The world was surprised at the rebels winning victory after
victory almost without effort—at Badajoz, Toledo, Talavera
and right on to Madrid. Anyone with even a slight knowledge
of the circumstances was, on the contrary, surprised that the
Republic should have survived the attack on it by its own
army.

All the way home I wondered why the General had never
removed his heavy military greatcoat, although there was a
grilling sun and the sweat was pouring down his face. Only
when I got back to the hotel did I learn the reason. He had
his greatcoat and uniform cap and his white cotton gloves—
but as yet no uniform.

On the 25th of January the news from the southern front
became alarming. The rebels had taken Marbella on the Gibraltar road and Alhama on the Granada road—two key positions. The fate of Malaga was going to be decided within the
next few weeks.

But it wasn't easy to get there. Railway communications
were cut and petrol rationed; two other journalists had been

waiting for days on end for an opportunity to get there. At last, on January 26th, we found one. The Press Department of the Ministry of Foreign Affairs provided us with a car and with petrol-coupons for two hundred miles. The distance to Malaga was almost five hundred, but it turned out that petrol became more easily available the farther one travelled southward from the capital.

There were four of us: Mrs. Gerda G., a Norwegian journalist; Mr. W., a Polish journalist; the driver and myself.

II

WE PASSED through Alicante on the night of the 27th and reached Almería, in the south, on the 28th. Here my diary of the last days of Malaga begins.

The notes, originally consisting of about twenty typewritten pages, were confiscated when I was arrested in Malaga; but in the prison at Seville I was able, while the dates were still fresh in my memory, to reconstruct them as accurately as possible, and to smuggle out this second version.

I leave unaltered these notes on the agony of a doomed city and the strange behaviour of the people who lived and died in it.*

Thursday, January 28th, Almería.

Got up, still depressed by talk yesterday with K. S. T. (a volunteer officer in the International Brigade) at Murcia. He said that during the Italian tank attack on the Prado front forty-two German Republican volunteers (some of them common friends) had been massacred in trench because they did not get order to retire in time. Useless and senseless holocaust. Red tape and negligence everywhere.

10 a.m. Saw Campbell, British Consul in Almería; following Spanish custom, palavered standing, without being offered a seat. Nevertheless was nice and helpful. Says Malaga will be terrible butchery. City believed able to defend itself to last man; says all foreign consuls have left Malaga because of constant aerial and naval bombardments. But British warships still in harbour—so still some hope of escape if cut off.

* A few paragraphs of the diary, omitted from the original edition, have been restored in the present edition.

Conversation cheered us up. These British consuls in forlorn Spanish cities are like pillars in the apocalyptic flood: dry and solid.

At noon go on towards Malaga. Road becomes worse and worse. Flooded at several points by streams of water coming down from the Sierras. Wonder how lorries with troops and ammunition can get through. As a matter of fact they don't get through; the road, the only road connecting Malaga with Republican Spain, is absolutely deserted. Is Malaga already abandoned? Yet we do not meet any refugees either. Very queer.

Motril, 3 p.m. Dirty little fishing village. No one knows where headquarters are. Finally we find them in the municipal school.

Fresh search for Commandant. At four p.m. we find him —an exhausted-looking youth with a five-days' growth of beard, a former postmaster and member of Prieto's Right-wing Socialist Party.

Shrugs shoulders in reply to our questions about absence of troops and arms supplies on road. Says, "Three days ago twenty lorries arrived in Almería with ammunition. They asked the local Syndicate to take the consignment on to Malaga because they had to go back.

"But the Almería Syndicate refused, saying it needed its own transport lorries for food supplies, and insisting that the Valencia lorries should take the consignment to Malaga. There was a row and the twenty lorries returned to Valencia; the munitions were dumped somewhere in Almería, and Malaga is without munitions. The rebels have only to walk in now. Maybe you'll meet them when you get there."

G. G. took notes, only to tear them up five minutes later. As a war correspondent you can't cable such things.

"By the way," said the Commandant, "you can't go on to Malaga. The bridge beyond Motril is broken. The road's flooded. You'll have to wait till the rain stops."

"So Malaga is practically cut off from the world?"

"As long as the rain lasts—yes."

"And how long has it been raining now?"

"Four days, and a wet period of ten days only ended last week."

"And how long has the bridge been broken?"

"Four or five months."

"Then why, in God's name, don't you repair it?"

Fresh shrugging of shoulders. "We get no material or specialists from Valencia."

The man's apathy exasperates me. I point out to him that Malaga's fate depends on this bridge—which he knows as well as I do—and say something about "criminal negligence."

The ex-postmaster gives me a long, untroubled look.

"You foreigners are always very jumpy," he says paternally. "We may lose Malaga, and we may lose Madrid and half Catalonia, but we shall still win the war."

There is a good deal of Oriental fatalism in the Spanish manner of conducting the war—on both sides; that is one reason why it seems to be at one and the same time so happy-go-lucky, cruel and rhapsodic. Other wars consist of a succession of battles; this one is a succession of tragedies.

An hour later we drive on, despite the broken bridge. It means a détour of about ten miles over practically impassable field paths, the last mile through the bed of a stream ten inches deep. Our light car gets through where a heavier vehicle would be water-logged.

Last stop before Malaga: Almuñécar. There is a once famous hotel here; Count Reventlow recommended it to us in Valencia. The hôtelier, a guileless fat man from Zurich, apologizes in German.

"You are my first guest for two months," he says. "I regret that you won't find my hotel as clean as usual, but you know there is a war on in Spain."

We say that we have heard so. After two hours of waiting we get an excellent dinner and drive on.

We arrive at Malaga about sunset.

First impression: a city after an earthquake. Darkness, entire streets in ruins; deserted pavements, strewn with shells, and a certain smell which I know from Madrid; fine chalk dust suspended in the air mixed with shell powder and—or is it imagination?—the pungent odour of burned flesh.

The straying lights of our head-lamps cast their gleam on piles of débris and yet more débris. *Pulvis et praeterea nihil*—Madrid after the great air attack and artillery bombardment was a health resort compared with this town in its death-throes.

In the Regina Hotel unprepossessing but good-humoured Militiamen are spitting on the marble pavement and eating the only available food—fried fish. We are the only guests in the hotel; the waiter tells us that this very afternoon a house nearby was destroyed by a 500-kilo. bomb, which killed fifty-two people in that one house alone.

The other waiters are gathered round the table discussing the air raid and everyone's reaction to it; how Bernardo hid behind the table, Jesús gazed out of the window, and Dolores, the cook, crossed herself fifty-seven times before she fainted.

I take a stroll with G. G. But the darkness is so menacing that we hurry back shivering and very uneasy. The porter looks at the star-lit sky, and remarks: "Fine air raid weather to-night." His daughter lost both her legs in yesterday's bombing and he wonders whether the bridegroom will take her without legs.

Friday, January 29th.

No bread for breakfast, nothing but black coffee; the food supplies of the town, like the munitions supplies, broken down as a result of irresponsible negligence; the damaged bridge at Motril has done its work, and the town with its 200,000 inhabitants is literally starving.

Busy all the morning visiting offices: Propaganda Department and Residence of the Civil Governor; come across goodwill everywhere, but hopeless red tape and lack of organization.

Impossible to get a message through; there are no censorship facilities for foreign journalists at all. After endless palavers we succeed in having a young officer with a slight knowledge of French appointed censor.

After lunch I go down to have a look at the harbour. Opposite the harbour is the British Consulate. There is quite a sizeable hole in the façade; a shell from a rebel cruiser dropped there without warning, but fortunately it did not explode. The English warship, too, is no longer moored in the harbour. Europe doesn't seem to be interested in the fate of Malaga.

A few men and women come running up from the harbour, their faces turned towards the sky. A moment later the bells begin to peal: an air raid warning. There aren't even any sirens. Everyone runs hither and thither in feckless confusion; the panic is much worse than it ever was in Madrid. The town is smaller; targets stand out more clearly against the sea; and the population is obviously demoralized. Incidentally a false alarm.

Later, interview with Colonel Villalba, officer in command of the Malaga forces. Admits frankly that things are going badly, but says that ten days ago, when he was appointed, they were still worse.

"I first inspected the most exposed front: the coast road Malaga-Marbella-Gibraltar," he tells me. "I found no trenches, no fortified positions, nothing but two Militiamen sitting smoking cigarettes a mile away from the enemy positions. 'Where are your troops?' I asked them. 'Somewhere in the barracks,' they replied. 'If the rebels were to attack, we should see them and have plenty of time to warn our men. Why should they sit out in the rain?' "

Go to bed filled with gloomy forebodings; try to persuade myself that it is all imagination.

Saturday, January 30th.

Visit to the Marbella front. Drive along the coast road; no sign of a sentry until, after about thirty-five miles, we are stopped at a barricade of stones; this is the "front." To the right of the barricade the Militiamen have begun to dig a trench; they sit around, their spades on their knees. G. G. focuses her camera. "Comrades," cries the Commander, "get busy. You are being photographed." He asks us what we "think of his front." I ask him what he proposes to do when the tanks arrive. He shrugs his shoulders. "I shall take my men up into the Sierra."

Sunday, January 31st.

Colonel Alfredo was supposed to be coming for us at 11 o'clock to take us to the Antequera sector. We wait for him in vain. At noon a Lieutenant of the Militia arrives and tells us that Alfredo is ill and that he has been detailed to take us to the front. We drive off about 4. I check our route by the map, for fear that we may take the wrong road and fall into the hands of the rebels. This may easily happen owing to the discontinuity and disorganization of the Spanish fronts. It has happened to a number of journalists; and even to quite a large number of officers on both sides.

After twenty minutes it becomes clear that we have taken the wrong road. The names of the places don't tally. I draw the Lieutenant's attention to the mistake. He smiles at the foreigner who always thinks he knows best. As usual not a sign during the whole drive of a sentry, a patrol, or anything to suggest we are near the front lines. At last we come upon two Militiamen marching along the high road. It transpires that we *have* taken the wrong turning; we are on the Alfernate and not the Antequera road, which we meant to take. The next village is six or seven miles away, and is called Colmenar.

I ask in whose hands Colmenar is.

"Ours," says one of the Militiamen.

"No, the rebels'," says the other.

The Lieutenant is furious. Finally we drive on to Colmenar. At the last curve in the road before the village we all peer out, our hearts thumping; what are we going to see—the green turbans of the Moors, or the black caps of the Militiamen?

Neither the one nor the other. There is no sign of any military personage in the whole of Colmenar. The front is seventeen miles farther on to the north.

The Lieutenant suggests taking a field-path, not marked on the map, across country to Antequera. It is already dusk. We mutiny and insist on driving straight on. We won't hear of any unfamiliar field-paths. After half an hour we reach the front at Alfernate. It looks somewhat more reassuring than the sector we visited yesterday. There are concrete pill-boxes on each side of the road. But the road itself is open. It runs straight on to the rebel positions, three miles away.

I ask the Captain in command of the sector why he hasn't blown up the road. He says indignantly that they would never do such a thing; they might need the road for a possible offensive. The pill-boxes on both sides would suffice to stop an advance on the part of the enemy infantry.

"And what about tanks?"

The Captain shrugs his shoulders. "Nothing's any use against tanks."

"All the same," I ask, "what are you going to do if they come?"

"We'll go up into the Sierra."

Monday, February 1st.

To-day at last we managed to visit the Antequera front, which we tried to reach yesterday. It is the most picturesque and the craziest front I've seen in this war.

Just as nearly everywhere in Spain, with the exception of the sector round Madrid, the "front" here too is synonymous with the high road. Now the high road Malaga-Antequera-Cordoba runs, just before passing through Antequera, over a high mountain pass. The mountain range is called Sierra el Torcal and is a spur of the Sierra Nevada. The pass is three thousand feet high. The ridge—sheer rock—looking down on the pass is about fifteen hundred feet above it. There, up above on the Devil's Rock, squats Captain Pizarro, gazing down at the road below to see if the rebels are coming. Beside him are a telephone and a steel wire. When the rebels come Pizarro is to telephone down to the post below. But as he is convinced that the telephone will fail to function at the critical moment, he has provided himself with the wire, which runs eight hundred yards to headquarters below; when he gives it a tug, a bell rings. Sometimes a bird comes and pecks at the wire, and then the alarm is sounded below.

This has been going on for six months; since the outbreak of the Civil War nothing has stirred in this picturesque sector but the clouds at Pizarro's feet as they drift from rebel into Government territory and thence back again.

Pizarro, by the way, claims to be a direct descendant of the conqueror of Peru. Six months ago, when he and his company first occupied this post, his men had neither blankets nor cartridges. The nights are cold in the Sierra, and at their feet lay the enemy town of Antequera, where there were sure to be cartridges and blankets in plenty. Captain Pizarro, feeling the blood of the Conquistadors in his veins, marched down one stormy night with a handful of men to Antequera, made a raid on the commissariat and came back with blankets and cartridges. Soon afterwards they ran short of cigarettes. So Pizarro raided Antequera and brought back cigarettes. Then came the spring and the peasants had no seed for sowing. The Alcalde made a solemn ascent to the Devil's Rock and suggested that Pizarro should make a raid on Antequera and bring back seed corn. And Pizarro made a raid on Antequera and brought back seed corn.

Never before had any journalists, let alone foreign journalists, turned up in this isolated outpost of the Civil War. The occasion was duly celebrated. We went down to the post below, where a sheep was slaughtered; as we were sitting down to our meal someone from above pulled at the bell and from the hill opposite a salute was fired.

Pizarro gleefully showed us all his treasures: a machine-gun (we each of us had to fire off a few rounds), his cavalry horses (two of them were led right into the peasants' living room where we were having our meal and they sniffed at the dish of mutton), and a chest full of hand-grenades (we were invited out of politeness to throw one, but we refused with thanks). G. G. in particular, charmed them, firstly because she was a woman, secondly because she was wearing trousers, and thirdly because she had a camera. She was given a present of a live kid; it is lying down beside my typewriter as I type these lines, bleating for its mother and quite unaware of the fact that it is a symbol; a symbol of the excessive good-nature and childishness of this people who have had Moors set upon them too. . . .

Yes, why indeed?

I really cannot think of any reason.

Of course I also asked Pizarro, obsessed as I was with my *idée fixe*, what he proposed to do if there should be a tank attack.

"Let them come," he said. "We shall strangle them with our naked hands, those devilish machines."

(*Postscript, London, Autumn.* They did come five days afterwards. I wonder whether Pizarro was killed outright or was merely executed later.)

Tuesday, February 2nd.

Wrote an article in the morning.

Midday paid a visit to Sir Peter Chalmers-Mitchell. He is the Grand Old Man of Malaga. In 1932, after having created the Whipsnade Zoo, the result of thirty years of planning, he bought a house here, to lead a peaceful and retired life. Peaceful indeed. . . . Adventurous spirits like him have a positive genius for getting themselves into a jam with the most innocent air in the world. He has just finished his memoirs, *My Fill of Days.* The well-cared-for house, half Spanish, half Victorian, and the neat garden, are just like an enchanted isle in this spectral town. We make friends at once; Sir Peter invites me to move to his house if the situation becomes critical. He is determined to stay on whatever happens. I have a vague feeling that I shall stay too. This town and its fate exert a strange and uncomfortable fascination over one. It is difficult to escape the spell.

Sir Peter has the same hungry look in his eyes as all the other inhabitants of this town. He lives on grilled sardines and biscuits and has to feed, in addition to cook, housemaid and gardener, the cook's daughter, the housemaid's aunt, the gardener's wife and mother-in-law; the whole tribe is lodged in the gardener's cottage, while the garage houses another twenty refugees from the neighbouring villages. Don Pedro— as they call him—lives amongst them like the old sheiks of a Beduin tribe.

Back at the hotel I fetched the kid from the bathroom—we had christened it "Joséphine"—and, after obtaining G. G.'s agreement, had it taken by the chauffeur to Sir Peter. Round Joséphine's neck we had fixed a strip of paper with a quotation from Plato's *Banquet;* all words signifying "Food,"

"Meal," etc., we underlined in red ink, as a discreet hint that the symbolical Joséphine was not to be sent to Whipsnade Zoo but to be well and truly eaten.

When I think over what I have seen on the various fronts, it all seems hopeless. But the strangest thing of all is the absolute quiet on all the fronts. Malaga is bombed from the air at least once a day; at the front not a single shot is fired. The last rebel attack was carried out on the Granada and Gibraltar roads simultaneously ten days ago; since that, nothing. I have a growing impression that for some reason impossible to understand, like so much else that is inexplicable in this bizarre war, the insurgents have given up the idea of attacking Malaga. I have had several talks with Villalba; he has the same impression. The town is still without food and without munitions; but it looks as though in some miraculous way it will be saved—a repetition of the miracle which saved Madrid in the days that followed November 6th, when the Caballero Government had fled to Valencia and Franco could have stepped into the Puerta del Sol at his leisure. By November 10th the defence had been organized and Franco had missed his chance.

After some hesitation I wire to the *News Chronicle:*
"Growing impression rebel offensive called off stop."

Wednesday, February 3rd.

Did some work, visited the Civil Governor, strolled about the town. At least fifty per cent of the town is in ruins. A veritable Pompeii. The other half, if possible, is in an even more wretched state. The majority of the shops, offices, banks, etc., are closed. The people in the street incredibly ragged, shabby, hungry, miserable. I am glad to be back in my hotel; we have moved to the Caleta Palace, which affords rather more protection against air raids. The hotel guests are mainly pilots. The one in the room above mine had his observer shot down yesterday. He sobbed the whole night long; there was a constant coming and going of comrades, trying to console him.

In the evening I learned at military headquarters that Queipo de Llano had begun a formidable offensive on the north-western sector. Nothing but grave faces at headquarters, general whispering, jumpiness. I have a feeling that the last act of the tragedy is about to begin.

What a fool I was to send off that optimistic telegram yesterday!

Thursday, February 4th.

The offensive began, surprisingly enough, in the sector Ardales—El Burgo, and—still more surprisingly—it was repulsed. Watched the fighting from a hill. Horrible butchery. Spoke to a deserter, Antonio Pedro Jiménez, from Dos Hermanos, near Seville. Says that there is a newly-established munitions factory, built and run by Italians; says ten to twenty lorries are transporting Italian infantry to the front all through the night.

In the afternoon paid a visit to Sir Peter; he has eaten Joséphine. His supply of cigarettes and matches is running low; he has divided them in rations to last for twenty days. But he still has some bottles of gin, Italian vermouth, and an excellent Spanish white wine. G. G. and I drank a lot on empty stomachs and felt rather exhilarated.

Nothing doing without alcohol. The pressure of outward events has to be balanced by a certain inward pressure; the brain remains lucid but stark reality is agreeably blunted. And one no longer minds.

Visited headquarters late afternoon, asked Colonel Alfredo how things were going. "*Ça va mal,*" he replied. "Enemy attacking simultaneously on all sectors." Asked how long he thought the town could hold out. Answered three days at most. Can't get any message past the censor.

Friday, February 5th.

Rebel cruisers "Canarias," "Baleares," "Almirante Cervera" and three smaller rebel warships bombarding all day along the coast north and south of Malaga. Where is the Republican fleet? Invisible. The rebels are unchallenged masters of sea and air. No food, no munitions. First symptoms of panic in the town. Learn that Civil Governor L. A. has deserted to Valencia. Last telegraph line destroyed near Motril. Try to get Marconigram through via Gibraltar but don't know whether my messages arrive in London.

At 5 p.m. impossible to obtain any news of the situation on the fronts. G. G. and I decide to drive along the coast to see for ourselves what's happening. We are the last journalists in Malaga; those of our colleagues who were here got away yesterday.

Reach Torre Molinos without a hitch. The C.O. there tells us it's not advisable to drive any further along the coast; the whole of Queipo de Llano's fleet is moored off Fuengirola and is blazing away at our front. The warships amuse themselves, he says, by picking out cars on the coastal road as targets. In the morning a Sergeant and three Civil Guards were hit by a shell from one of the ships as they drove along in a car. "There wasn't that much of them left," he says, pointing enthusiastically to the black beneath his nail.

We leave G. G. in Torre Molinos and drive on, the driver and I. We pass through Fuengirola; just beyond it there's a bend and a bay. In the bay lie, drawn up in a beautifully straight line, the "Baleares," the "Almirante Cervera" and three smaller warships, scarcely a mile from the shore, and they fire salvos, just as in fleet exercises. Not a battery to answer them. A machine-gun barks in impotent rage from the coast.

We leave the car behind some bushes and proceed on foot. Beyond the next bend a whole column of lorries with provisions and munitions is drawn up. The drivers have refused to drive any further, "because it is too dangerous." The front, that is, the miserable barricade of stones we saw a week ago, has been twenty-four hours without supplies. It's really laughable to think that Queipo has to bring five warships into action to shell these wretched positions. Obviously he overestimates the defence.

The road now runs directly along the shore. Inland there is an escarpment, and behind it a company of Militia is concealed. It is posted there to prevent a possible attempt on the part of the rebels to effect a night landing to the rear of the front. They order us to duck. If a head is visible from the ships, they will immediately start peppering us over here. The ships lie directly opposite us, but they fire obliquely at the "front," which is about a mile farther on.

It's all just like a film. One has a feeling one is looking right into the muzzles of the guns. First one sees a spurt of flame, then the smoke, then one hears the detonation, then the whistle of the projectile, then the impact and the explosion.

It is the sheerest target practice.

After about ten minutes the fleet begins to steam slowly towards Malaga, hugging the coast. The shells fall nearer; 500, 200, 100 yards. It is a veritable inferno. We cling to the ground with every limb, make ourselves as flat as flounders. We don't even dare to whisper—just as if we could be heard on the ships. The last hit covers us with a rain of clods. Then the.shots become less frequent and the fleet steams past.

On the "front" everything is quiet. It doesn't exist any longer. Logically the rebel infantry ought to advance now. But it is dark and Spaniards don't like attacking in the dark. Probably they won't attack until first thing in the morning.

In the evening Colonel Alfredo comes to dinner with me at my hotel. Says Alfernate and Ventas de Zefareya lost; that means the end.

G. G. says she will leave to-morrow. Then I shall be the last of the Mohicans.

Saturday, February 6th.

Several air raids during the morning. No news from London since Thursday, so feel certain my messages are not getting through. Went to Civil Governor's Residence, as I wanted to find out whether I could use radio for S O S message telling the world that Italian troops are going to capture Malaga. But at the Governor's Residence they've all lost their heads. Went to military headquarters with same object, but Villalba is invisible and has left orders that *la presse—la presse, c'est moi* —is not to be allowed to cable anything about the military situation except optimistic propaganda stuff. Army people always imagine that if they call a defeat a victory it *is* a victory and the dead will arise. They believe in the magical effect of lying propaganda just as bushmen do in the prayers of the witch doctor.

In the meantime G. G. has got ready to leave. An official is taking her in his car to Valencia. I have just time to scribble a few words on a scrap of paper for her to phone from Valencia to the Foreign Editor of the *News Chronicle:* "Malaga lost. K. staying. Try to obtain appointment of Sir Peter Chalmers-Mitchell as acting honorary Consul so that he may mitigate the slaughter."

About 2 p.m. the exodus from Malaga begins. The road to Valencia is flooded with a stream of lorries, cars, mules, carriages, frightened, quarrelling people.

This flood sucks up everything and carries it along with it: civilians, deserting Militiamen, deserting officers, the Civil Governor, some of the General Staff. From the arteries of Malaga it sucks all its powers of resistance, its faith, its morale. Nothing can resist its magnetic force. The road to the east has become a road for one-way traffic. Nothing more coming through from the capital; no munitions, no food, no organizer, no saviours—although even now it is not too late.

Nobody knows the fate of this stream once it is lost beyond the first bend in the road to the east. Odd rumours go the rounds in Malaga: the rebels have already occupied Vélez, the next town to the east, about thirty miles away; the stream of refugees is flowing into a death-trap. According to another rumour the road is still open, but under fire from warships and aeroplanes, which are mowing down the refugees with machine-guns. But nothing can stop the stream; it flows and flows, and is incessantly fed from the springs of mortal fear.

At 4 o'clock I decide to have a look at what is happening in Vélez. My driver, although he is a former Militiaman, is infected by the panic; he tries to persuade me to drive on through Vélez to Valencia and not to come back. To calm him I tell him that we will decide when we get to Vélez. As the car drives off I see that all our luggage is stowed away in it, although I have given no orders for this to be done.

We let ourselves be carried along by the stream to the little fork that branches off from the coast to the north. The town of Vélez itself lies some miles inland. The road is still open. We drive into Vélez.

Vélez is in a state of chaos. The Militiamen of the routed army lie sleeping on the pavements, in doorways, under the marble tables of the cafés. They have lost all soldierly shape—they are dirty bundles of clothes with shivering creatures inside. Those who are not asleep hang about at street corners, rolling cigarettes, waiting for the arrival of the executioners. These men are done for. They have tried to keep off the advancing tanks by throwing stones. A fox hunt has been going on—human foxes and a motorized hunt. Those who were caught alive struck out with knives; and when their hands were bound they bit.

Our car is immediately surrounded by a group of Anarchist

Militiamen. "This car is requisitioned." "What for?" "To dynamite the bridge on the road to Ventas." "But I've been told that the bridge has already been blown up." "Shut up and get out of the car." After a little palavering I persuade the Anarchist leader to come with me to military headquarters. It is deserted. A solitary Civil Guard is killing flies in the courtyard. "Where is the Commandant?" "If you want to see the Commandant you must address a written request to him." "Are you mad? The rebels are only three miles from the town." "You're joking. The rebels are fifty miles to the north, the other side of Ventas." "Can't you hear the machine-guns? That's the rebels." When the man at last realizes that we are speaking the truth, he reacts in an odd way: clutching his head with both hands, he runs off and vanishes. The Anarchist, I don't know why, runs after him and also vanishes.

We ask everybody where the Commandant is; nobody knows and nobody cares. At last we find him in a restaurant—he looks dog-tired and has apparently not slept for at least two days; he is listening calmly to three Militiamen, who all speak at once, gesticulating wildly, while he carefully peels himself an orange.

"If you are a newspaperman look around you and you won't need to ask questions." "What about the bridge to Ventas?" "We blew it up an hour ago." "How long will it take to build a temporary bridge?" "Twelve hours." "And then?" No answer. The Commandant shrugs his shoulders and peels a fresh orange very carefully. Then he asks: "Are you going back to Malaga?"

The driver: "No, to Valencia."

I: "Yes, back to Malaga."

"Then please take my Political Commissar with you to Malaga. I have no car. Maybe he can get some munitions for us." "No munitions in Malaga either." "I know. Still——"

We hurry away. The driver is completely unnerved. He complains that somebody has stolen his cigarettes out of the car while we have been talking to the Commandant. The Commissar asks him whether he has nothing better to worry about at this moment; and he answers, pale, stubborn: "No."

We fight our way against the stream back to Malaga. All the way back the Commissar declaims optimistically: Vélez will hold out, Malaga will hold out, our brave Militiamen won't retreat an inch, etc. He is twenty-five and has been a member of the Socialist Youth from the age of eighteen. He knows all about the situation, and he knows that I know all about it, and that to-morrow the entire world will know about it even if I don't cable a word. But his grey matter, soaked with propaganda, is proof against all realization of the truth.

As soon as we get back to Malaga, and stop at headquarters, the driver declares categorically that he won't stay any longer. Indeed, I have neither the right nor the power to keep him; I only ask him to take my luggage from the hotel to Sir Peter Chalmers-Mitchell's house, since the critical moment seems to have arrived. Twenty minutes later driver and car disappear along the Valencia road, and with them the last chance of getting away.

It is dusk now. I feel very lonely and abandoned, and sit down on the steps outside headquarters. Colonel Alfredo comes along and sits down beside me. After a while he says: "This is probably our last night. The road will be cut off in a few hours, and they will kill us like rats in a trap."

"What are you going to do if they come?"

He taps his revolver. "I've still got five cartridges. Four for the Fascists, the fifth for myself."

I have an uneasy feeling that he is acting a part, and that Alfredo and the Commandant of Vélez and the Anarchist and the Civil Guard and all the others, including myself, are children playing at being Walter Scott heroes and are unable to visualize the stark reality of death.

It is completely dark now; uninterrupted grumbling of cannon and coughing of machine-guns behind the hill.

Alfredo takes me to the officers' canteen. I fill my pockets
with dry bread and two bottles of cognac. Then I stagger
through the pitch dark city to Sir Peter's house, with the
Union Jack planted on its white roof.

Sunday, February 7th.

Breakfast air raid at 8 a.m. The noise of artillery and
machine-guns incessant now. Later on another air raid. One
of the planes, a white monoplane, swoops scarcely a hundred
feet above the house, screaming and scattering bullets. Lola,
Sir Peter's housemaid, has hysterics.

We climb the hill opposite to get a good view. We can hear
the bombardment more clearly, here and there we can see
white puffs of smoke, but it is impossible to gain a clear picture of the strategic position.

On our way back we see thick smoke pouring out of the
windows of the house next to ours. The house, lying in the
midst of a large park, belongs to a rich Spaniard, who after
the outbreak of the Civil War fled abroad with the help of
Sir Peter. Now it is used as a temporary hospital. After a time
the smoke becomes less dense and then stops entirely. Obviously the building has not been set alight by a bomb, but by
a chance conflagration. To think that such a thing is still
possible. . . .

After lunch—lunch is an exaggeration—went into the town.
Since yesterday the physiognomy of the town has changed;
no more trams, all shops closed, groups at every corner and
every face shrouded in the grey cobweb of fear. Brilliant sunshine, the sky a glaring blue, but the wide wings of death are
outspread and envelop the town. Just as I am passing Caleta
Bridge a squadron of six rebel planes flies very low above our
heads, sowing murder. I look for shelter beyond the bridge;
there are two Militiamen drinking cognac, one singing the
"International," the other in a low voice and with a stupid

smile, the hymn of the *Falange*. I feel the contagion of fear getting me too.

Reach headquarters; it looks like a night refuge; inhuman-looking men asleep on desks and floors. While I wait to be received by Colonel Villalba, an exhausted sergeant staggers in and is conducted straight to the Colonel. I enter with him.

"What news?" asks Villalba.

"They are coming down the Colmenar road with fifteen tanks."

"How far are they?"

"An hour ago they were five miles from the city."

"Resistance?"

"None. Our people threw away their rifles and made off to the Sierra."

"Thank you."

The sergeant slumps down under a table and immediately falls asleep. Villalba has a short whispered conversation with some of his staff officers. An order is given to an aide-de-camp and they leave the room rather hurriedly.

I stop Villalba. "What do you want?" he says nervously. "Can't you see I'm in a hurry? I can give you the following statement: The situation is critical, but Malaga will put up a good fight."

"Where are you going?" I ask him. But he is already gone.

I rush to a window and look down. Villalba and his staff officers are getting into a car. Everybody is looking rather embarrassed. The car leaves the courtyard.

"Where is he going?" I ask an officer whom I know.

"He has deserted," the officer says calmly.

"It was his duty to leave," says another one. "We shall be cut off in an hour, and he is the Commanding Officer of the entire southern sector; so he had to leave."

"How can he command if we are cut off?"

"He has deserted," repeats the first one.

"Who is boss now?" I ask.

"Boss?" Everybody looks surprised. Nobody knows.

I go into another room. There is Colonel Alfredo sitting at a typewriter. It is all like a bad dream. I note that he is using the red half of the ribbon. I read:

"To all whom it may concern. This is to certify that Colonel Alfredo G. is leaving on an important mission to Valencia. Authorities are requested to let him pass.

"You too, Alfredo?" I ask him.

He blushes. "And you, too. I'll take you in my car. It's all up."

This is no longer Walter Scott. I feel the ants of fear creeping over my skin.

In the courtyard we find X. a common friend. He is ill; a high temperature, coughing and spitting.

"Come," says Alfredo, "it is all over."

"Go to hell. I'm staying," says X.

"Villalba has left too. We'll take you by force," says Alfredo, tears in his eyes.

"Go to hell," says X. (He is dead now. Eighty per cent of the persons mentioned in this story are dead.)

We step into Alfredo's car. Alfredo's mother is in the car, and Alfredo's sister and some other women, all crying and sobbing.

When the car starts I remember Sir Peter; during the last hour I have completely forgotten him.

"We must take my English friend," I say to Alfredo.

"Impossible," says the driver, "the Fascists are on the New Road; his house is cut off."

"But I only left him an hour ago!"

"They've entered the town since. Can't you hear the machine-guns?"

I hesitate. We reach the city barrier. The crowd of refugees stares at us, privileged owners of a car, with envy and hatred.

A feeling of deep disgust suddenly comes over me; my nerves are all to pieces.

"Stop," I say to the driver, "I want to go back."

"Don't stop," says Alfredo.

I jump out of the car. Alfredo gesticulates wildly. The car disappears in the crowd.

It is dusk again. I walk back slowly to Sir Peter's house. The rebels are not yet here.

They did not come until the next day.

III

THEY came on Monday afternoon.

But as yet it is only Sunday. There is yet time to get away. It is dusk, and the sombre, flaccid shadows of the Andalusian night are rapidly closing in. No electric light; no trams; no policemen at the street corners. Nothing but darkness, and the death-rattle of a strangled city: a shot, a drunken cry, a whimpering somewhere in the next street.

Militiamen run through the streets, demented, aimless. Women in black mantillas flit along like bats in the shadows of the houses. From somewhere or other comes the sound of splintering glass, the window of a car.

It may be half an hour ago that I jumped out of Alfredo's car and began to wander about the streets. There is no longer anyone in control, anyone in authority; there are no public services left in the city; its very bones have gone soft, its nerves, sinews, muscles, are decomposing, the highly developed organism has degenerated into an amorphous jelly-fish. What is the agony of an individual compared with the agony of a city? Death is a natural biological process, but here a whole social organism, the very foundations of civilization itself, is out of joint. The taxpayer reverts to the state of cave-dweller, and in his short-sighted eyes behind their horn-rimmed spectacles lurks primitive fear.

On this Sunday night, the seventh of February, nineteen hundred and thirty-seven, a new St. Bartholomew's Night is being openly prepared. An army of foreign invaders is encamped beyond the hills, recouping its strength in order, to-morrow, to invade these streets and drench them in the blood of people whose language they do not understand, with whom they have no quarrel, and of whose very existence they were yesterday as unaware as to-morrow they will be indifferent to their deaths.

There is perhaps still time to get away.

Sir Peter's house is on a hill half a mile outside the town. I wander across the dark fields and find myself outside the park gate of a large, villa-like building. I assume it is the hospital we saw burning early this morning. Now it is dark and deserted, an enchanted castle. I knock for a long time on the door of the porter's lodge; after a while the porter appears, grasping a revolver. His whole body trembles and the revolver trembles with it.

"Is this the hospital?"

"There's no hospital here."

"What is this house, then?"

"This is Señor Bolín's house."

Bolín—the name is familiar to me, disagreeably familiar: Bolín, the rebel Press chief in Seville. A most uncommon name in Spain. The coincidence, if coincidence it be, increases my uneasiness. I ask the porter if he knows where "Don Pedro's" house is. He points with his revolver to the left.

"There—just next door."

"But if it's next door, then this *is* the hospital."

"This isn't a hospital. It *was* a hospital. But from to-morrow on it will be Señor Bolín's house again."

So that's how things are. The man no longer trembles; he now obviously feels he has got the upper hand of me. He slams the door in my face; but while I am still standing there irresolutely, his wife comes out with a lighted candle and leads me across the fields to Sir Peter's garden. Either this is common human kindness or else the couple are, after all, not quite so sure what the morrow may bring. In such situations even the simple-minded become diplomats.

Sir Peter is sitting at his writing-desk in the light of an oil lamp, apparently oblivious of what is going on outside—a perfect Victorian idyll in the midst of the apocalyptic flood. I feel rather like a Job; moreover, I feel conscience-stricken because I am late for dinner and my clothes are dirty—on the way here there was another air raid and I had to grovel among the furrows.

Solemnly, by candlelight, we eat our grilled sardines and drink Sir Peter's excellent Spanish white wine. Lola, who has a sense of humour, serves our four rachitic sardines on an ornamental silver dish; she too seems to be acting "The Last Days of Pompeii"; but her eyes are red.

We talked over our prospects; they did not look too good. Sir Peter had published two letters in *The Times* attacking the Rebels, and had engaged in open propaganda in favour of the Spanish Government in England; his sympathies for the "Reds" were generally known. As to myself, certain adventures at Seville, to which I shall refer later, had led the Rebel authorities to issue a warrant for my arrest, and the book which I had just published in Paris certainly did not make me more popular with Generals Franco and Queipo de Llano. To offset this list of sins there was only one argument in our favour: the Union Jack on our flag pole. But it was not a very triumphant-looking argument just now. Its edges were frayed by the weather, and it hung limp and rather helpless in the wind.

"Look here," said Sir Peter, "I'm not going to run away. There are two hundred thousand people in Malaga. To-morrow, when the rebels come, they may possibly shoot fifty thousand. All the Consuls have gone, the world takes no interest in Malaga, they can do whatever they like here. If they know that I am here, a 'neutral observer', so to speak, perhaps they'll shoot only forty thousand. And even if my presence makes no difference I want to stay, and, if I survive, tell the world what happened to Malaga. Never yet, either in Badajoz or in Toledo, has a foreigner been a witness of the things the rebels do when they enter a conquered town. I think it is worth while staying for that."

Then he tried to persuade me to leave him alone, arguing that I was more compromised than he.

Whereupon I tried to make him see that I could not possibly leave him alone—after all, he was a man of seventy-three and I a man of thirty-two. Despite the solemnity of the occasion, this was an argument that was not to dear Sir Peter's taste.

In the intervals of conversation we sipped the white wine; Lola changed the candles, and with a grand air served us each with a spoonful of raspberry-jam; and it was really all rather like the last days of Pompeii.

Then we went out on to the terrace and saw in the distance beyond the dark hills a row of shining points of light, like a chain of fairy lamps at a fête, which seemed scarcely to move; they were the rebel tanks coming down the mountains from Colmenar. The sight of them sobered us a little. Sir Peter went to his room and came back with two small metal cases, which looked like Gillette razor sets. Each contained a hypodermic syringe, with a spare needle and a tube of morphine tablets.

"Look here," said Sir Peter, "I have seen the illustrations in your book"—he meant the photographs of Franco's tortured and mutilated victims—"and I don't like the thought of it. It might be useful to have one of these on you."

Then he explained to me with scientific thoroughness how to use a hypodermic syringe. The tube contained sufficient tablets to enable one to escape from all the horrors of all wars, civil and otherwise.

"One must disinfect the needle over a flame, of course, before giving oneself an injection," explained Sir Peter, "or one may get an abscess."

I remarked that in the situation in question an abscess more or less would hardly make any difference. Sir Peter said that my remark was logically unassailable.

I went straight into the bathroom and practised giving myself subcutaneous injections. Through the window I could see the fairy lights of the tanks slowly drawing nearer, and yet I had a feeling that I was carrying out a perfectly absurd and silly experiment, the sort of thing for which my father used to threaten to spank me.

Afterwards we switched over to gin and vermouth and wise and philosophic conversation. From the town isolated shots rang out, and we heard the occasional abrupt bark of a machine-gun. Our great ambition was to ignore these disturbing sounds and refuse to allow them to spoil our chat. There was obviously a certain element of snobbishness in our attitude, and I think Sir Peter was as aware of this as I; but we both probably felt that in our present situation a little snobbishness was excusable and even indicated.

The next day Malaga fell.

We breakfasted as usual at eight o'clock. Usually the bombardment did not begin till nine—Spaniards sleep late even when making war—and we wanted at least to finish our porridge in peace.

But we were not to be allowed to. At our second mouthful three warships loomed on the horizon, outlined against that sea which lay stretched out there below the terrace, so revoltingly innocent and indolent and blue; and these warships were making full steam ahead for the harbour.

They came rapidly nearer, steering a straight course. When they were no more than a mile away, the bombardment, we knew from experience, would begin. But they did not open fire. Trailing their smoke-banners behind them, they made straight for the still Republican port of Malaga.

Could it be that at last the warships from Carthagena had come to our aid? For the space of a moment we thought so; for the space of a moment believed in the possibility of a miraculous rescue at the eleventh hour; then we saw through the glasses the enemy flag, the red-yellow-red flag of the Monarchy.

Shortly after nine the cruisers steamed into the harbour of Malaga. We were still waiting for them to open fire.

But they did not fire. The coastal batteries were silent, the guns of the cruisers were likewise silent, and their flags hung down limply from the masts. That was all.

We no longer understood what was going on. We no longer knew what was happening down below there in the silent city.

But we assiduously entered up our diaries.

Monday, February 8th, 1937 (the day on which Malaga fell).

8 a.m. During breakfast observe through glasses rebel cruisers, flying red-yellow-red Bourbon flag, entering port of Malaga. Waiting for bombardment to begin, but they don't open fire.

8.30 a.m. Eight rebel 'planes hovering above us in the sky. But they drop no bombs.

9 a.m. Usual hour for artillery bombardment to begin. But not a single detonation. Sunshine, and dead, ghostly silence.

9.30 a.m. A straggling, ragged swarm of Militiamen streams down from the Colmenar high road. Most of them no longer have rifles. All have bearded, exhausted faces, and the hopeless, furtive look of the hunted. None speaks. Some stumble. They march past the house without looking up, and vanish round the bend in the road.

10 a.m. An isolated straggler—a wounded Militiaman, unarmed and half dead with exhaustion, passes by the house and asks for water and cigarettes. As I give him a light, I can see his hands and feet trembling.

"Is the road to the town still open?" he asks.

"Yes, still open."

"They won't kill me?"

"They won't kill you."

"Are you sure they won't kill me?"

"I am sure they won't kill you."

"God bless you, Señor."

And he staggers on.

(I wonder whether they did kill him.)

11 a.m. Rebel cruisers and 'planes continue to disport themselves in the waters and in the air of still Republican Malaga.

Sir Peter and I decide to go into the town to find out what is happening.

Immediately we leave the house an invisible machine-gun begins to bark in the neighbourhood. The road is under fire. We walk back.

12 a.m. A refugee family enters the garden—a man and wife, two children, and a mother-in-law, with a vast array of baskets and packages, chiefly containing bedding. (There is a touching conventionality about the way in which in all great catastrophes—fires, floods, wars—the poor and wretched rescue their bedding before everything else. Next in the hierarchy of earthly treasures come pots and pans and household crockery. This order of selection of the goods they consider worth saving is perhaps the starkest and most shameless revelation of the permanent misery of the masses of this world. Third on the list comes usually the cage with the canary, the pet cat, or a preposterous mongrel dog; they stand for the sunny side of existence.)

The family take up their quarters in the garden. We greet them in our customary way, with clenched fist—the usual greeting in Republican Spain—but they keep their hands still and smile sheepishly. We ask them where the rebels are, and the woman says in a whisper, and with a sly wink:

"The National troops are everywhere in the hills—here—there." And she lays a finger on her lips as though there were Moors hiding behind the bushes.

We ask her what things look like in the town, and she replies, still whispering, and with the same sly wink:

"Ever since this morning there has been a white flag on the Civil Governor's Residence."

IV

So IT is all over. Malaga has surrendered.

And I remember Colonel Villalba's last statement before he stepped into his car: "The situation is a critical one, but Malaga will put up a good fight."

Malaga did not put up a good fight.

The city was betrayed by its leaders—deserted, delivered up to the slaughter. The rebel cruisers bombarded us and the ships of the Republic did not come. The rebel 'planes sowed panic and destruction, and the 'planes of the Republic did not come. The rebels had artillery, armoured cars and tanks, and the arms and war material of the Republic did not come. The rebels advanced from all directions, and the bridge on the only road connecting Malaga with the Republic had been broken for four months. The rebels maintained an iron discipline and machine-gunned their troops into battle, while the defenders of Malaga had no discipline, no leaders, and no certainty that the Republic was backing them up. Italians, Moors and Foreign Legionaries fought with the professional bravery of mercenaries against the people in a cause that was not theirs; and the soldiers of the people, who were fighting for a cause that was their own, turned tail and ran away.

The guilty leaders of the town, who deserted their men, were court-martialled. The guilty government of Largo Caballero, who left Malaga to her fate, was forced to resign. The guilty governments of the Western Democracies, which left the Spanish Republic to her fate, could neither be court-martialled nor forced to resign; they will be tried by History. But that will not make the dead arise.

The longer one waits for a thing to happen, the more astonished one is when it finally does happen. We had known for days that Malaga was lost, but we had pictured the end differently. Everything had proceeded so terribly silently, noiselessly, undramatically. Events had shown every sign of coming to a head, but we were cheated of the climax. In all secrecy the white flag had been hoisted on the Malaga tower. When, on the morrow, the enemy's cruisers and 'planes arrived, we expected them to open fire, and did not realize that there was no longer an enemy, that we were already living under the domination of the Bourbon flag.

This smooth, slick transition was more terrifying than anything we had feared. Without our knowing it, while we slept, we had been delivered up to the tender mercies of General Franco.

The entry of the rebel troops likewise took place in an uncannily natural and undramatic fashion. My diary runs:

1 p.m. An officer wearing the grey steel helmet of the Italian army appears on the road leading to Colmenar, just opposite our house.

He looks round and fires a revolver shot into the air. Immediately after this about two hundred infantry come marching down the road in perfect formation. They are singing Mussolini's hymn, "Giovinezza."

As they pass by the house they salute us, and the household staff, who only yesterday assiduously raised their clenched fists, now, with equal Spanish effusiveness, raise their arms in the Fascist salute. They seem perfectly at ease, but since they look upon us foreigners as half imbecile, the gardener advises Sir Peter and me to change our demeanour, too, "because we have a new Government now."

After some time, as more and more troops go by and salute us—we are all gathered on the balcony as though reviewing a march past—Sir Peter and I are constrained to raise our arms too. We avoid looking at each other.

I drink a tumblerful of cognac.

2 p.m. A company of Italian infantry occupies the neighbouring hill.

3 p.m. The Italian Lieutenant in command of the company on the hill comes into the garden and asks whether he may wash. He introduces himself courteously, and Sir Peter gives orders for a bath to be got ready for him. A few soldiers follow him down from the hill to get a wash and a drink of water. They do not speak a word of Spanish. They look pretty worn-out; their behaviour is perfectly polite.

Sir Peter and I settle down in our deck chairs on the porch. The sun is shining. We hear the Lieutenant splashing about in the bathtub. We agree that he is a nice fellow. We still avoid looking at each other.

Shame chokes me, is like a dry sponge in my throat.

4 p.m. A storm of hurrahs and clapping is heard coming from the city. The rebels have reached the centre of Malaga.

4.30 p.m. Cars flying the Bourbon flag come driving along the road. Tanks are lumbering down in an endless column from Colmenar. Shots can be heard from the town at regular intervals. One of the household staff volunteers the suggestion that, since the fighting is over, these shots may mean "that the execution of the Red criminals is beginning."

Once more it was evening, and once more we sat opposite one another on high-backed Victorian arm-chairs at the formally laid table.

I had burned all compromising papers: letters of introduction from the Spanish Embassy in Paris, travel-permits issued by the authorities at Valencia, and all the copies of my book except the one which I had dedicated to Sir Peter; but he promised to destroy that too. Then I blotted out all dangerous references in my diary.

They might come for us at any moment now—it was most likely that they would come at night—but we did not really believe it. In the morning, when I had given the trembling

Militiaman his cigarette, I had still had one last impulse to flee. I had half resolved to fetch my typewriter and papers from the house and join the Militiamen. And it was mainly out of indolence that I had not done so. Down below in the town all was chaos and uncertainty, and the garden here basked so peacefully in the sun—it seemed highly improbable that things of a disorderly nature could ever happen in this neat and well-kept garden.

I was reminded of a scene from a play about the French Revolution by a German writer of the last century. Danton learns that Robespierre is going to have him arrested on the following day, and he flees from his house at night. He wanders blindly across the dark heath. It is cold and windy, and suddenly he has a feeling that it is highly illogical to be wandering at night over a windy heath instead of sleeping at home in his good bed. Robespierre and the Convention seem to him unreal figments of the imagination, and the only common-sense thing to do seems to be to go home to bed and sleep. This he does. "Even should we know in theory," is the substance of his reflections, "even should we know in theory of all the dangers that threaten us, deep down in us there is a smiling voice which tells us that the morrow will be just as yesterday." The next morning he is arrested.

Deep down in us, too, on this last evening was that smiling voice that told us that the morrow would be just as yesterday.

The next morning at 11 a.m. we were arrested.

V

AT THIS point the story becomes slightly entangled and strange coincidences crop up; I must go back to the past.

In August, 1936, the first month of the Civil War, I had visited Portugal and rebel Spain for the *News Chronicle*. In Seville, at that time the insurgents' G.H.Q., I had an interview with General Queipo de Llano and ample opportunity to observe the amount of German and Italian military support for the insurgents. The evidence I collected was published by the *News Chronicle*, and later in the book which I have mentioned (*L'Espagne Ensanglantée*). Never again was a representative of a British liberal paper allowed to enter rebel territory.

During my stay in Seville, Captain Bolín, in charge of the insurgents' Press Department, had acted as my cicerone. It was Bolín who had arranged my interview with General de Llano.

On the day after that interview I met a German journalist whom I had known years before in Berlin. His name was Strindberg (a son, by the way, of August Strindberg, the great Scandinavian writer), and he was now working for Nazi papers. He was actually sitting with four Nazi pilots in the lounge of an hotel in Seville when we met. He knew all about my "Red" past, which was unknown to Captain Bolín. The same evening he denounced me to him.

I managed to escape to Gibraltar just in time; the warrant for my arrest was issued an hour after I had crossed the frontier. Back in London, I published my material. Colleagues coming from Spain told me some months later that Captain Bolín had sworn "to shoot K. like a mad dog if he got hold of him."

It was this same Captain Bolín who arrested Chalmers-Mitchell and myself the day after the insurgents occupied Malaga.

Yet this is only one half of the prelude to our story. The other half runs thus:

Captain Bolín had a cousin. This cousin had a house in Malaga. It was the villa next to ours. The cousin's name was Señor Thomas Bolín. This Thomas Bolín and his entire family owed their lives to Sir Peter. Sir Peter told me how this had happened during the last dinner we had together in his house, on the night before we were arrested.

Thomas Bolín was a member of the *Falange*, the Spanish Fascist party. On July 18th, 1936, the Generals launched their insurrection throughout Spain. In Malaga, as in Madrid and Barcelona, the rebels, after fierce street fighting, were defeated; the Republicans remained in control of the city, and Señor Bolín came to the house of his neighbour, Sir Peter, whom he knew to be a "Red," to ask for shelter and protection.

He arrived with his wife, mother-in-law, five or six children and two or three maids. Sir Peter installed the whole Bolín tribe in his house. Señor Bolín occupied the same two rooms which I was to live in six months later. On his arrival he handed over certain documents for safe keeping in an envelope which Sir Peter locked away in a drawer of his writing-desk.

The next day an Anarchist patrol visited the house.

They did not wish to trouble Sir Peter, knowing his sympathetic attitude towards the Republican Government, but they demanded to see the documents of the Señor living upstairs.

Sir Peter was obliged to hand over the documents. The Anarchist leader, a young lad, opened the envelope. The first thing he found was Señor Bolín's Phalangist membership card, the second a set of pornographic pictures such as are posted to amateurs by certain bookshops in Paris. The Anarchist seemed highly delighted with both discoveries. Then Sir Peter had one of his usual happy inspirations.

"Look here," he said in his smoothest tones, "we'll strike a bargain: you keep the pictures, and I'll keep the card."

The Anarchist, who, as I have said, was very young, was at first indignant, then amused, and finally, out of friendliness towards Sir Peter, he consented.

Some days later, nevertheless, Señor Bolín was arrested. But Sir Peter secured his release, obtained passports for his family, and finally, at the peril of his own life, smuggled Bolín out of Malaga to Gibraltar.

Bolín's luggage remained in Sir Peter's house; Bolín's villa was converted into a military hospital.

We were arrested on Tuesday, February 9th, at 11 a.m.

At 10.30 I was standing on the roof, our usual observation post, counting the lorries full of Italian troops which were still driving down from the mountains in an endless column. The Italians looked fresh and well-fed. Their faultless equipment, from steel helmet to puttees, provided a striking contrast to the ragged, wretched garb of the Republican Militiamen. As their radiant, good-humoured faces, the happy faces of victors, appeared, one after another, in the field of vision of my glasses, I tasted the bitter feelings of the poor man in the fable who is invited to dine at the rich man's table.

Then I saw an elegant private car, covered with dust and decorated with the Bourbon flag, driving up the road to Señor Bolín's house. I told Sir Peter of this.

"Perhaps it is Bolín returning from exile," he said. "It is *his* turn now to protect *us*."

And he walked over to the villa.

Ten minutes later he returned, pale and upset.

"It *was* Bolín," he said. "He's just come back by car from Gibraltar."

"Has he got any more dirty postcards?"

"No, but he's wearing the red beret of the *Requetes*, and has a huge army revolver. He says it will give him great pleasure to hunt down the Reds in the town and kill a few of them with his own hands."

"Did he at least say 'thank you' to you?"

Sir Peter shrugs his shoulders and goes upstairs to get Señor Bolín's belongings together for him.

I am left alone in the garden. Once more I feel in urgent need of a drink of brandy, and I go into the library to get one.

The library has three doors. While I am looking for the brandy, the three doors open simultaneously, almost noiselessly, and three officers, revolvers in their hands, enter. Two of them are unknown to me. All I notice is that they are wearing brand-new uniforms.

The third is Captain Bolín.

What follows happens very quickly, just as in a speeded-up film. The syringe is in my pocket; all I require is to be left alone for two or three minutes. Acting quite automatically, I try to slip upstairs. When I get to the third stair a sharp voice calls me back.

"Hands up!"

I raise both hands above my head, without turning round, and wait for Bolín to shoot. At the back of my skull I feel a faint itching, a sort of sucking void, not entirely unpleasant. It increases from second to second; I hear all four of us breathing loudly.

"Come down."

I step down backwards with great care. "If I stumble," I think to myself, "I am a dead man."

We stand in a group in the middle of the library; three revolvers are pointed at me—one from each side, a third from the rear.

It is all very dreamlike, the air hums round me as in the hollow of a sea-shell. Through the humming I hear Captain Bolín's voice, calling to the gardener:

"A rope."

The gardener goes off to fetch one. I notice that he is limping.

Sir Peter appears at the top of the staircase with Señor Bolín's valise in his hand.

"Hands up."

He puts his hands up. But he stands erect.

There is silence for a few seconds. We all stand in a frozen group, like wax-work figures at Madame Tussaud's.

Then a fourth individual, with a red cap, enters the room. I recognize him at once by his resemblance to his cousin; it is Señor Thomas Bolín. He stands looking on at the pleasant little scene with a grin on his face.

"Sir Peter," I ask, "is this the man whose life you saved?"

Señor Bolín grins.

The gardener comes back. He has been unable to find a rope, but has brought two yards of electric wiring.

"I believe they're going to hang me," I say to Sir Peter.

It occurs to me that the final agony will be certain to last longer with this inflexible wire than it would with an ordinary rope.

"Shut up!" says Bolín. And he makes a sign to the officer on my left.

The officer—a handsome young man who looks rather shy and seems to be quite a nice fellow—takes the wire and plants himself behind me. He twists my hands behind my back and tries to bind them with the wire. But the wire is too stiff. He walks round me, pulls my hands round to the front as though manipulating a wooden doll, and once more tries to tie them.

Meanwhile Bolín is pressing a revolver into my right side, the third officer a revolver into my left. This latter is a fat, bald-headed fellow with incredibly bestial features. During the whole proceeding he has a grin on his face and literally snorts with pleasure. He snorts through his nose as though he has asthma; I can feel his breath on my ear. Up till now I have only come across such sadistic types in political cartoons, and have never believed that they actually exist. The fellow grins, and snorts and snorts. He is obviously a pathological case. My physical disgust breaks the dreamlike spell, I am fully conscious again and fear returns; it creeps under the skin and grips the entrails.

Then, to my own astonishment, I hear myself saying:

"Look here, Bolín, if you're going to shoot me, take me upstairs; don't do it in Sir Peter's presence."

Later on I often wondered whether this sentence, which may have saved my life, was prompted by consideration for Sir Peter or merely by the desire to gain time. Perhaps it was a mixture of both motives; but I rather think the second predominated.

"Shut up!" says Bolín; but there is a trace of uncertainty in his voice.

The next thing I remember is Sir Peter reasoning with Thomas Bolín. He was asking if he could have five minutes' conversation with him in the next room. Señor Bolín smiled sardonically, but in the end he gave in. The two of them went into the next room. Captain Bolín supervised the complicated procedure of the binding of my hands, and then joined them. The door was left ajar. The three had a short palaver. It was obvious from their gestures that Sir Peter was pleading for me, but just as obvious that he was not having much success.

I was not allowed to go near them.

"What's happening?" I shouted through the open door.

They came out, and Sir Peter said very quietly:

"It seems that it is all right for me, but not for you."

Then we were taken away.

To this day I do not know what made Captain Bolín abandon the idea of shooting me out of hand: whether my words had made him realize the responsibility he would be taking upon himself if he were to shoot a foreign journalist in a house flying the Union Jack; or whether the gentleman with the red beret and the filthy pictures had after all brought himself to the point of intervening.

It is an elevating thought that one should owe one's life to a set of dirty postcards.

VI

THEY took us out to a car. My hands were bound, Sir Peter's were not. Thomas Bolín had disappeared. The car drove off. Beyond the bend of the road we were stopped by a detachment of soldiers; they knocked on the window-panes with their fists and seemed quite prepared to lynch us. But Captain Bolín persuaded them that this would not be a nice thing to do, and we went on.

We stopped in front of the police station. On the flag pole a brand-new red-yellow-red banner had already been hoisted. Captain Bolín and the fat officer got out; Sir Peter and I had to remain sitting in the car, guarded by the younger officer who had bound my hands.

We waited for two hours. The sun was shining and it was extremely hot. I can't remember what we talked about; I expect most of it was nonsense.

The whole time I could see in my mind's eye the photographs in my book of people being tortured. I asked Sir Peter in English whether, as we had agreed, he had destroyed the autographed copy of the book which I had given him. He said that he hadn't been able to bring himself to do so. This was bad.

"The only thing I am afraid of is being tortured," I said to Sir Peter.

"I don't think they'll torture you," said Sir Peter. It occurred to me that he spoke in the same tone of voice as that I had used to the wounded Militiaman when he had asked me whether I thought that he would be shot. Then Sir Peter began to recite to me certain lines of Swinburne which he

51

knew I was very fond of, and which appear on the flyleaf of
his recently published memoirs.

> *"Pray thou thy days be long before thy death,*
> *And full of ease and kingdom; seeing in death*
> *There is no comfort and none aftergrowth,*
> *Nor shall one thence look up and see day's dawn*
> *Nor light upon the land whither I go.*
> *Live thou and take thy fill of days and die*
> *When thy day comes; and make not much of death*
> *Lest ere thy day thou reap an evil thing."*

He spoke very quietly. The young officer looked at him in
surprise. I realized that he meant this as a kind of last Sac-
rament.

Then we were separated.

Bolín and the fat officer came back and took Sir Peter away
with them. I did not think I should ever see him again.

As for me, the first thing they did was to photograph me
in the street, first full face, then in profile. A crowd stood
about, cracking the usual jokes. It was very humiliating, but
Sir Peter's quiet voice still echoed in my ears:

> *". . . and die*
> *When thy day comes; and make not much of death."*

These peaceful lines were very comforting, and gave me
a feeling of superiority, almost of contemptuous arrogance.
Then they took me into the police station.

While we were crossing the forecourt an officer of the
Phalanx prodded me on the chest. "*Ruso, Ruso*—a Russian,
a Russian!" he exclaimed in the excited voice of a child which,
when taken to the Zoo for the first time, shouts: "A crocodile, a crocodile!" I said that I was not a Russian, but he
wouldn't listen to me.

"To-night you'll be flying off to your Moscow Hell," he said with a grin.

I was led into a vast empty room. In the corner of the room was a stool, upon which I was made to sit down. Two Civil Guards sat down opposite me near the door, their rifles on their knees.

We sat like this for a while.

Then I heard screams coming from the courtyard, and a young man, his naked torso streaming with blood, was led into the room. His face was battered, cut about and slashed; for a moment I thought the man must have been run over by a steam engine. Holding him by the armpits they dragged him across the room. He yelled and whimpered. The Phalangists who were dragging him along spoke to him in honeyed tones: "*Hombre*, we're not going to beat you any more." The door closed after them, and a moment later there were sounds of ringing blows and dull thuds and kicks. The man groaned and cried by turns. He cried at regular intervals.

Then for a few seconds there was silence. All I could hear was quick, stertorous breathing. I don't know what they did to him in those few seconds. Then he screamed again in an unnaturally high-pitched shrill voice; and then at last he was silent. A few moments later the door flew open and they dragged him across the room in which I was sitting into the courtyard. I couldn't make out whether he was dead or merely unconscious. I did not care to look very closely.

Then a second victim was taken through the room to be subjected to the same treatment; and then a third.

Every time they went through the room the Phalangists looked at me as though marking me down as their next victim, but they said nothing. After the third case, no more were brought in; I sat still and waited.

The Civil Guards sitting opposite me seemed to be disagreeably affected by these proceedings. While the tortures were going on in the next room they scrutinized my features keenly to watch my reaction; perhaps, too, with a faint stirring of pity. When the third victim was brought back, dead or unconscious, the elder of the Civil Guards shrugged his shoulders with a glance in my direction; it was an unconscious gesture of apology. In it was expressed the whole attitude towards life of a fifty-year-old gendarme who, on the one hand, had thirty years of service in a medieval country behind him and, on the other, probably had a wife, several underfed children and a pet canary. In it was expressed an entire human philosophy of shame, resignation and apathy. "The world's like that," he seemed to be saying, "and neither I nor you will ever change it." The shrug of the Civil Guard is more vivid in my memory than the screams of the tortured.

I sat on the stool in the corner of the room for a very long time—for several hours, in fact; maybe two, maybe three or four. It took me half an hour to summon up the courage to get up and pace up and down. At first the Civil Guards growled at me and I sat down again; but after another half an hour or so I got up again, and this time they raised no objection. They smoked and chatted. I had a definite purpose in mind, and pursued it with the patience and obstinacy of an old lag; it is astonishing how quickly one picks up such things. My idea was, while pacing up and down, surreptitiously to take the hypodermic syringe, the two needles and the tube with the morphine tablets out of their case and to secrete them in various parts of my clothing. Slowly and patiently I succeeded in doing this; I slipped the syringe into my packet of cigarettes, the needles into the inner lining of my coat, the tube into my breast-pocket handkerchief. At this point I asked to be taken to the lavatory; I needed some water to dissolve the tablets.

After a short consultation they acquiesced. They allowed me to close the door but not to bolt it. It was a real Spanish lavatory; there was no tap, but only a wretched puddle on the flagstones. I began to fill the syringe from it, but such a wave of disgust came over me that I stopped and came out again.

It was dark by the time Captain Bolín and his fat friend came back.

They took me out into the courtyard, and Captain Bolín gave orders for me to be thoroughly searched.

Two soldiers set about this task. First of all my pockets were emptied. The fat officer went through my pocket-book. I had burned any papers that might be compromising, and my pocket-book now contained only a few personal documents, some money, and two telegrams from the Foreign Editor of the *News Chronicle* on technical matters, asking me, amongst other things, to send all photographs by air-mail.

"What kind of photographs does he mean?" asked the fat officer.

"Why, Press photographs," I said in astonishment.

"Since when has it been the practice to send Press photographs by air-mail?" he asked scornfully. Like so many officers, he obviously had an espionage complex; and mistrust combined with stupidity and malevolence are about as dangerous a mixture of qualities as you can find in a man. I realized that it was hopeless to argue with him, and merely shrugged my shoulders—and even that, for safety's sake, only in imagination.

Then happened what was only to be expected.

The soldier who was feeling the lining of my coat let out a terrified yell and clapped his thumb to his lips; he had pricked it on the hypodermic needle.

"He's got something sharp hidden in the lining," he said, sucking in rage and fright at his thumb.

I pulled out the needle and held it up in the half light of the courtyard.

"What is that?" shouted the fat officer, recoiling several paces. Bolín, too, stepped back. They were all convinced that they were at last being confronted with the famous needle containing Indian snake venom which they knew so well from films and detective stories. It was a positively awesome moment.

I was made to deposit the needle on a plate, for they all refused to touch it. Then they examined my cigarette packet, and discovered the syringe. They shook out my handkerchief and discovered the tablets, and finally I myself voluntarily produced the second needle from the lining of my coat. I was obviously the most dangerous individual that had ever trodden Spanish soil—Mata Hari and Madame X were only wretched amateurs in comparison.

Bolín counted over my loose cash; then he made me sign a receipt which ran:

"This is to confirm that I had 700 French francs and 150 pesetas on my person at the time of my arrest."

He put the receipt in his pocket. The meaning of this proceeding was obvious. Bolín wanted to obtain from me a sort of posthumous testimonial to the businesslike correctitude of his behaviour.

I had on me, in addition, a few small Catalan banknotes, which are of no real value in rebel territory.

"You can keep those," he said, "they'll do to pay your fare when you set out on your journey to Heaven to-night."

I asked them to leave me my fountain-pen.

"You won't need that in Heaven," he said, and handed it over to his fat friend, who tested the mechanism with obvious satisfaction. The pen was a present from my wife. I don't care much for symbols, but the thought that my old pen, which I had used to write my first book on Spain, should fall as booty into the hands of a Fascist officer was particularly galling to me.

When they had finished searching me, all that I had left was my wrist-watch, which they had fortunately overlooked.

I was taken back to the room, dark by now, and again hours went by. I paced up and down, the rifles of the Civil Guards before my eyes, with a feeling of utter hopelessness. I had eaten nothing since breakfast, but didn't feel hungry. About 10 p.m. a non-commissioned officer came and ordered me to be put into a lorry. Five men took their places behind me, their rifles on their knees. I was convinced that I was going to my execution.

The lorry drove off. The streets of fallen Malaga were as dark as before. Soldiers were camped everywhere: Moors with their grubby green turbans, Phalangists and Foreign Legionaries. But no Italians were to be seen in the town; the rebel leaders obviously attached no importance to parading the national liberators before the eyes of the civilian population. In any case the civilian population apparently preferred to celebrate their liberation behind closed shutters.

The passage of our tumbril evoked the usual jeers from the soldiers. I tried to discover in what part of the town we were —I assumed that the execution, as is customary, would take place in the cemetery, and puffed away furiously at the last but one of my English cigarettes. At this moment I felt neither excessive fear nor any other feeling except a wish that it might all be over as quickly as possible and without torture. I calculated that they could not possibly aim straight in the dark, and that they would therefore place me in front of the lorry's headlights or finish me off with a revolver shot as I alighted. This latter seemed to me an ideal way of dying; but out of superstition I did not dare to hope for it.

Finally I summoned up enough courage to ask a soldier. He said in quite matter-of-fact tones that I was not going to be shot yet, but taken to prison. Then he took a light from my cigarette and said to the man behind him:

"This fellow thought he was going to be shot straight away."

"Rot," replied the other, whose face I could not see, in a good-humoured booming bass. "Rot. It's not such a quick business as all that, *hombre*."

We drove up to the prison, and the driver rang the night bell. That a prison should have a night bell is quite logical, but somehow it seemed odd to me. The great iron door opened, and we marched down a long, ill-lit corridor into the office. I was searched all over again, and made to strip down to my underclothes. One official tapped the soles of my shoes with an iron hammer, another passed his hands through my hair. Having an aversion to sock-suspenders, I always wear golf stockings, and the official asked me whether I had ever disguised myself as a woman. Once again I had to grin in spite of my despair.

"*Lleva calcetines de mujer,*" (wears women's stockings), the official wrote in my record. As he was doing so, I managed to catch a glimpse of the record that had been made out by Captain Bolín and was lying on the table in front of the official. I read that I was a very dangerous character—I presume that was because of the hypodermic needle—that I should be most carefully guarded and kept *incomunicado*—that is to say, isolated; and that I was a *caso internacional*—an international case—or spy.

And now, to crown all, came the "women's stockings." The chain of evidence was complete.

Finally my finger prints were taken, and I was allowed to put all my clothes on again with the exception of my belt, which was kept in the office.

Then I was taken to a cell.

For the first time I heard the sound of a cell door being slammed from the outside.

VII

It is a unique sound. A cell door has no handle, either outside or inside; it cannot be shut except by being slammed to. It is made of massive steel and concrete, about four inches thick, and every time it falls to there is a resounding crash just as though a shot has been fired. But this report dies away without an echo. Prison sounds are echo-less and bleak.

When the door has been slammed behind him for the first time, the prisoner stands in the middle of the cell and looks round. I fancy that everyone must behave in more or less the same way.

First of all he gives a fleeting look round the walls and takes a mental inventory of all the objects in what is now to be his domain:

>the iron bedstead,
>the wash-basin,
>the W.C.,
>the barred window.

His next action is invariably to try to pull himself up by the iron bars of the window and look out. He fails, and his suit is covered with white from the plaster on the wall against which he has pressed himself. He desists, but decides to practise and master the art of pulling himself up by his hands. Indeed, he makes all sorts of laudable resolutions; he will do exercises every morning and learn a foreign language, and he simply won't let his spirit be broken. He dusts his suit and continues his voyage of exploration round his puny realm— five paces long by four paces broad. He tries the iron bedstead. The springs are broken, the wire mattress sags and cuts into the flesh; it's like lying in a hammock made of steel wire. He pulls a face, being determined to prove that he is full of courage and confidence. Then his gaze rests on the cell door, and he sees that an eye is glued to the spy-hole and is watching him.

The eye goggles at him glassily, its pupil unbelievably big; it is an eye without a man attached to it, and for a few moments the prisoner's heart stops beating.

The eye disappears and the prisoner takes a deep breath and presses his hand against the left side of his chest.

"Now, then," he says to himself encouragingly, "how silly to go and get so frightened. You must get used to that; after all, the official's only doing his duty by peeping in; that's part of being in prison. But they won't get me down, they'll never get me down; I'll stuff paper in the spy-hole at night. . . ."

As a matter of fact there's no reason why he shouldn't do so straight away. The idea fills him with genuine enthusiasm. For the first time he experiences that almost maniac desire for activity that from now on will alternate continually—up and down in a never-ending zig-zag—with melancholia and depression.

Then he realizes that he has no paper on him, and his next impulse is—according to his social status—either to ring or to run over to the stationer's at the corner. This impulse lasts only the fraction of a second; the next moment he becomes conscious for the first time of the true significance of his situation. For the first time he grasps the full reality of being behind a door which is locked from outside, grasps it in all its searing, devastating poignancy.

This, too, lasts only a few seconds. The next moment the anæsthetizing mechanism gets going again, and brings about that merciful state of semi-narcosis induced by pacing up and down, forging plans, weaving illusions.

"Let's see," says the novice, "where were we? Ah, yes, that business of stuffing paper in the spy-hole. It *must* be possible to get hold of paper somehow or other." He leaves the "how" in this "somehow" suspended in mid-air. This is a mode of thought that he will soon master—or, rather, it will master him. "When I get out," he will say for example, "I shall never worry about money again. I shall rub along somehow or other." Or: "When I get out, I shall never quarrel with the wife again. We'll manage to get along somehow."

Indeed, "somehow or other" everything will be all right once he's free.

The fact that the prisoner follows this stereotyped line of thought, which, as I say, is going, after a few days, completely to master him, means that the outside world increasingly loses its reality for him; it becomes a dream world in which everything is somehow or other possible.

"Where were we? . . . Oh, yes, that business of stuffing paper in the spy-hole. Of course, somehow or other one can get hold of some paper. But is it allowed? No, it's certain not to be allowed. So why bother? . . .

"Let's take a more thorough inventory of the objects in the room. Why, look, there's an iron table with a chair which we haven't observed or fully appreciated yet. Of course the chair can't be moved from the table; it's welded to it. A pity, otherwise one might use it as a bed table and put one's things on it when getting undressed—pocket-book, handkerchief, cigarettes, matches and so on . . ."

Then it occurs to him that he has neither pocket-book nor handkerchief, cigarettes nor matches in his pocket.

The barometer of his mood falls a second time.

It rises again the moment he has tried the tap over the wash-basin. "Look, there's running water in prison—it isn't half as bad as one imagined from outside. After all, there is a bed (and it's much healthier to sleep on a hard bed), a wash-basin, a table, a chair—what more does a man need? One must learn to live simply and unassumingly: a few exercises, reading, writing, learning a foreign language . . ."

The next voyage of discovery is in the direction of the water closet. "Why, there's even one of these—it's really not half so bad." He pulls the plug. The chain refuses to function. And the barometer falls afresh.

It rises again once the subtle plan has been conceived of filling the bucket with water from the tap and of flushing the lavatory pan in this way. It falls again when it transpires that the tap has also ceased to function. It rises again when he reflects that there must be certain times of the day when the water runs. It falls—it rises—it falls—it rises. And this is how things are to go on—in the coming minutes, hours, days, weeks, years.

How long has he already been in the cell?

He looks at his watch: exactly three minutes.

I said that I am convinced that the vast majority of prisoners behave in this or some such way during the first few moments of their imprisonment. The more drastic a situation, the more stereotyped the way in which people react to it. Whenever life is at its most dramatic, it is least able to escape the commonplace. At the so-called great moments of life, we all behave like characters in a penny novelette. The virtue of the word lies in the sphere of abstractions; before the concrete and tangible language pales.

It becomes a completely useless instrument when it is a question of describing such horribly ordinary and naked facts as the fear of a human being in the face of death.

I had hardly been five minutes in the cell when there was a rattling in the lock and the door was thrown open.

Outside stood the two officials I had already met, the one who had searched me and the one who had entered the bit about the "women's stockings" in my record.

"*Venga,*" they said. "Come."

I did not dare to ask where.

Once more we marched down the long, bare corridors, past an endless row of closed cell doors.

To every spy-hole on each side of the corridor a goggling eye was glued.

We passed through a double file of eyes—of wide-open, staring eyes, eyes without people attached to them.

The warder who had searched me was in radiant mood. He stretched out his hand in the direction of this and that cell, giving a downward sweep with his index finger.

"Bang, bang," he said. "Reds, Reds, the whole lot of 'em. All dead to-morrow."

The eyes stared. Behind each hole was a pupil.

"You dead to-morrow, too," said the warder.

I had a feeling that my knees were nothing but flabby jelly. "The condemned man walked with an uncertain gait." All condemned men walk with an uncertain gait. Damn those penny novelettes.

At the end of the corridor was an iron grille. The official turned a lock and threw the grille back. Behind it was a shorter corridor with a few cells: the isolation cells.

One of the cell doors was unlocked: I was given a thump in the back and hurled in.

And once more the door slammed to behind me.

The fixtures were exactly the same, only the barred window was smaller and placed somewhat higher up. The wall above the iron bedstead was spattered with blood. It must have been fresh blood, for it still smelt slightly sour. I smelt it and then I was sick.

I felt utterly wretched. I lay down on the wire mattress. There was no straw palliasse and no blanket. It was bitterly cold. I was freezing, the iron network cut into all my limbs, and I could not escape that sour smell. The W.C. was blocked and the tap did not function. Through the window I could hear isolated shots, then a salvo, then shots again, and, in between, cries. They were piercing yells which ensconced themselves in the labyrinth of the ear and remained there long after the yelling man was silenced for ever. I had to be sick a second time. I lay on the bed, reduced to a bundle of misery. "Now you are nothing but a bundle of misery," I thought, and could not help grinning. Then it occurred to me that they had taken away my belt but not my tie. Above the bed was an iron hook for clothes, and I thought that really the most sensible thing to do would be to put an end to all this unpleasantness. The hook was placed very low, but I remembered having often read in the papers that middle-aged clerks, on losing their jobs, have a predilection for hanging themselves on door-handles. That hook was anyhow no lower than a door-handle. I experimented a little but I found that it was a distinctly unpleasant procedure, and gave it up. After that I felt an odd relief. I was happy to breathe again the stinking air of the cell; I suddenly felt very sleepy, and did not care about anything else. I slept soundly and peacefully until dawn.

When I awoke I did not know where I was, and when I remembered I did not feel any the better for it. A few grimy rays of light filtered through the grimy window. Utter, bleak silence reigned. It is only in prisons that the air is so deaf.

It always requires resolution to get up in the morning. This morning there was nothing to get up for; no work awaited me, no post, no duties. For the first time I experienced that curious feeling of freedom and irresponsibility which is one of the will-o'-the-wisp-like illusions of prison psychosis. I turned over on my wire mattress, pulled my legs up to my stomach to keep myself warm, and felt like a schoolboy playing truant. Then I dozed off again.

When I awoke, the light was still uncertain; a sound had awakened me. I listened; someone was singing. It sounded fairly near. The man who was singing must be in one of the isolation cells opposite. I sat up and felt my heart stand still: the man was singing the "International."

He was singing it all out of tune in a hoarse voice. He was obviously waiting for the other condemned men to join in.

But no one joined in. He sang all alone in his cell, in the prison, and in the night.

I had read descriptions of German prisons and concentration camps. The singing of the "International" as a political protest or as a last demonstration was frequently mentioned in them; but despite my profound respect for the German martyrs, such passages had always struck me as a little melodramatic and improbable. Now I myself was hearing a man who knew that he was going to die singing the "International." It was not melodramatic at all; the hoarse, unmelodious voice sounded wretched and pitiable. He repeated the refrain two or three times, dragging it out to make it last longer, to delay the moment when silence would return. I got up and posted myself by the door, and, my teeth chattering, raised my fist in the salute I had learned at meetings in Valencia and Madrid. And I felt that in the adjoining cells all the others were standing at their doors like myself and solemnly raising their fists in a farewell salute.

He sang. I could see him before me, with his unshaven, battered face and tortured eyes.

He sang. They would hear him outside and come and tear him to pieces.

He sang. It was unbearable. How we all loved him.

But none of us joined in the singing—fear was too strong.

VIII

THE first day in prison began; the first of one hundred and two days.

There was no breakfast, no water for washing, no comb to comb my hair with. There was nothing to do but wait. I paced up and down, six and a half paces up, six and a half paces down, trying hard to think of pleasant things and to be an amusing companion to myself. The first thing that occurred to me was a quotation from one of Edgar Wallace's Sanders Stories.

". . . We've only got to die once. Personally speakin' that never cheered me up. If you died more than once you'd get used to it, old Ham. Do you see my meanin'? That's philosophy."

That *was* philosophy, I thought. And I was surprised to find how difficult it was to think of cheerful things; indeed, to control the direction of one's imagination at all. If one lets go only for a second, the helm slews round on its own.

I took a piece of wire out of the bedstead and began to scrawl mathematical formulæ on the wall. I worked out the equation of an ellipse; but I couldn't manage the equation of a hyperbola. The formulæ became so long that they reached from the W.C. to the wash-basin. I gave it up and looked at my watch. It was one o'clock. Only then did I realize how hungry I was; I had eaten nothing for twenty-nine hours.

I flew into a rage and began to hammer on the cell door; at first with my fists, then, taking off a shoe, with that. I had seen a man do this in an American film. Unfortunately my shoes were rubber-soled.

Nothing stirred. My rage evaporated, and once more I grew apathetic. I pressed an eye to the spy-hole and peered out into the corridor. I could only see a small section of it; my field of vision was just large enough to take in the door immediately opposite. But after a while I made an exciting discovery; the spy-hole opposite mine kept lighting up and growing dark again at regular intervals.

Since the cells were lighter than the corridor, the hole was normally a white spot. It was obvious that, when the hole grew dark, my opposite number also had his eye glued to it. But all I could see was that the hole grew dark; I could not see the eye.

The intervals lasted only a few seconds; it was unlikely that the man could be peering out, turning away and then peering out again with such regularity. It seemed probable that he was trying to signal to me.

I began to cover up my spy-hole with my hand and un-cover it again at the same regular intervals. Then I slowed down the tempo, then accelerated it. But there was no change in the rhythm opposite. Now I placed a finger right over the hole; at first horizontally, then vertically. I did this three times, and then stopped, for it occurred to me that I had been making the sign of the cross.

But my *vis-à-vis* did not react. The light and the darkness alternated, still at the same regular intervals, with depressing monotony.

I racked my brains to make out what the man was getting at. He could not produce this effect merely by pacing up and down, for the intervals were too short. And suddenly I had it; I knew what the man was doing, I could *see* it physically before me.

He was standing with his legs straddled in front of his cell door and swaying his head from side to side, right, left, right, left, like a nodding bear. He must have been in the very last stages of apathy and despair.

I knocked on my door. I made all kinds of shapes with my fingers against the spy-hole. No reaction.

This got me down again. Once more I lay down on the bed and dozed off. I tried to recite poems to myself, but my mind had ceased to function. The helm was refusing to obey.

About four o'clock there was a noise in the corridor. An oily voice read out a list of forty to fifty names; doors flew open and were slammed to again. A trampling of feet, whispering, mysterious sounds. This time I put my ear instead of my eye to the spy-hole. All I could discern was that a long file of men was shuffling through a corridor somewhere, slowly and hesitantly, as though walking against their will. The trampling died away. Forty to fifty men were marching to their death.

I lay on my bunk and wondered whether the singer were amongst them, whether they were shot one by one or in batches; with rifles or machine-guns. My imagination, no longer under my control, depicted for me the scene outside, in all possible variations, fifty or a hundred times.

I was gripped by an obsession: I was convinced that if I managed to visualize the scene in all its detail, I would prevent its accomplishment; that the imaginative anticipation of an event could annul its chances of realization.

But at the same time—and without noticing the contradiction—I felt an equally obsessive urge to share mentally the fate of the others and go over and over again in my imagination the scene of their execution. I thought it would make dying easier for them. And some half-conscious, cunning hope made me also believe that this act of solidarity would be rewarded and that I would be spared.

All this time I kept looking at my watch, and at five o'clock I said to myself: It is all over for them by now. I lay on my bunk exhausted, my eyes were burning, I covered my head with my jacket. I wished I could pray for the dead and for myself, and hummed the "Marseillaise" into the lining of the coat, without shame.

Shortly after five I was fetched from my cell. A warder whom I had not yet seen asked me whether I knew a "certain Mitchell," and whether I knew where he was. He spoke in quite a kindly manner. He took me to the office, where several Phalangists and an officer were sitting about, and said in vexed tones: "*He* doesn't know where the Englishman is, either."

The officer gave orders for the official and me to search the prison for "Mitchell."

From which it became clear to me that they had not even a complete list of the names of their prisoners. To be a "Red" was quite enough; what did the name matter? Mass graves need no inscriptions.

We wandered through the labyrinth of corridors and courtyards. First through the courtyards; there were three or four of them, and they were all cram full of men waiting to be shot, Militiamen, peasants, and people from the working-class districts. They stood about in groups or sat on the ground, smoking. They were all unshaven; they all had the same leaden, hollow-eyed gaze, the same flickering, hunted look in their eyes as they glanced up at the warder and me. They must have taken me for an informer.

"Can you see him?" the warder whispered in my ear. I replied that I could not.

Taking me by the arm, the warder led me into the middle of the courtyard. There was a clear space all round us. I could feel that they thought I was an informer. I could feel their hatred, and I looked down at the ground. "Don't be afraid," shouted the warder. "We haven't come for anyone this time. Is there anyone among you who is an Englishman and is called Mitchell?"

No one replied, and we went on to the next courtyard. There were three or four courtyards; and each presented the same picture. I estimated that there were fifteen hundred to two thousand men in the prison. That makes ten thousand bullets, I calculated, and about seventy thousand unlived years.

Then we looked into one or two cells. In some of them, which were no bigger than mine, five to six men had been herded. There was no room to lie down; they sat side by side on the floor, as though in a railway carriage, waiting for the end of the journey.

We also passed the cell of my *vis-à-vis;* this corridor contained only isolation cells occupied by single prisoners. I asked the warder who the man was. He looked at me in astonishment. "Who should he be? Why, a Red, like you." At the end of the corridor we met an elegant young officer. Stopping us, he asked us whether we had found Chalmers-Mitchell.

The warder replied in the negative.

The officer asked me in broken English whether it was true that Chalmers-Mitchell was "an English aristocrat."

"I should just think he *is,*" I said. "He is a member of a very old aristocratic family, and a great friend of the King." I said this so convincingly that the young officer turned quite pale. Determining to make the most of the situation, I introduced myself and said that I regretted that I was obliged to make his acquaintance in such an unshaven state.

He was slightly taken aback, and announced his own name: "Franco."

He almost gave me his hand.

I asked him if he could arrange for me to be taken before the court in order that the mistake with regard to my arrest might be cleared up as quickly as possible.

He said that he had no say in such matters, but that the National Army never made a mistake.

I said that in time of war there must surely be occasional

exceptions. It certainly could not, for example, be the express intention of the National Army that I should have been left without food for thirty-six hours.

"Aha!" he said, with a sarcastic smile, "so you've gone on hunger strike."

I replied that I was not on hunger strike, but had been given nothing to eat. But that was of no importance; the important thing was that I should be given a hearing.

He shrugged his shoulders, and I quickly tried to change the subject before he left us; I asked him with polite interest whether he was related to General Franco.

Whereupon he flushed crimson, turned his back on me and walked off.

"*Vamos*," said the official, grinning. "We must go on."

We went back to my cell. I was about to say something more, but he banged the door in my face.

This exciting episode was over, and I was alone once more.

About seven o'clock I heard the sound of shuffling feet and a great clatter and din in the corridor. I rushed to the spyhole. Two warders were dragging along an enormous tub, about the size of a baby's bath, with a brown liquid in it. It was coffee. Two others were carrying a huge basket of bread.

The cell door opposite was opened, and at last I set eyes on my *vis-à-vis*, the bear. At first all that I could see in the half-light was the bearded lower part of his face and a tattered shirt, stiff with congealed blood. He was standing in the corner of the cell furthest away from the door, his back pressed against the wall, his hand raised defensively in front of his face.

"*Hombre*," said the warder who was carrying the ladle, an amiable old fellow, "we're only bringing the coffee. There's no beating here in prison."

He filled the ladle with coffee and handed it to the bear, who put out both hands for it and gulped down its contents with terrifying avidity. He gulped and smacked his lips; it sounded just like a dog drinking. The four warders stood looking on. Then one of them handed him a hunk of bread from the basket. The man pressed the loaf against his shirt and gaped at the warders, that same hunted, half-crazy look still in his eyes. He panted audibly. Then, obviously after a struggle, he asked:

"There won't be any more beating?"

"Not here in prison," said the old warder.

He was about to shut the door when my *vis-à-vis* pressed his outstretched hand against it and asked:

"When . . . ?"

This was all he managed to get out.

The old warder shrugged his shoulders and closed the door.

The coffee and bread procession continued on its way from cell to cell of the row opposite. My field of vision was only wide enough to take in the bear's cell; but I could hear them coming along my row from the end of the corridor. Shortly before they reached my cell, a fifth warder came up with an armful of tin drinking vessels—old tinned-food containers and little petrol cans.

I was given my tin full of coffee and my hunk of bread. But I had long since been considering whether it would not be better, now that I had already gone thirty-six hours without food and drink, to go on fasting and so weaken my powers of resistance as much as possible. While I had paced up and down, the screams of the tortured victims in the police station had continued to ring in my ears, almost as vividly as though I were the victim of a hallucination. If it comes to it, I thought, the weaker one is, the quicker one will lose consciousness.

So I poured the coffee down the W.C., and the bread too, after having broken it up into little pieces. In doing so, I had the impression that I was again taking an active part in the course of events, that I was putting up some sort of fight; and this thought had a calming effect. I crouched on my wire mattress and tried to go to sleep.

I must have dozed off when the oily voice that I had heard in the morning woke me up again.

This time it came through the barred window from one of the courtyards through which I had wandered in my search for Sir Peter. It read out twenty-five to thirty names. I could not count them exactly; the long Spanish names confused me. This time all those whose names were called out had to answer "present," and if the answer did not come promptly, the oily voice burst forth into a flood of abuse. Then it called out:

"All those from Cell No. 17."

"All those from Cell No. 23."

These were the nameless ones, who were shot and buried anonymously. And they could not even say: *"Eli, eli, lama sabachthani."*

The oily voice rose up twice more that night; once about midnight—sixty names—once shortly before dawn. The last time it came from a distant wing of the prison, an indistinct, faint murmur; I could not keep count.

Then another day dawned.

It was Thursday now, not yet forty-eight hours since I had been a free man, able to open doors with my own hand, comb my hair, wash, blow my nose, and ring for the maid to bring me a drink.

About ten o'clock the "bear" was taken out of his cell.

This time no names were read out. A warder and two soldiers approached the cell at a businesslike pace. The warder swung the door open and called out to the inmate: *"Valor, hombre"* (Courage, man), and hurried on to the next cell; the soldiers seized the bear, bound his hands and led him away out of my field of vision. Three more times I heard that *"Valor, hombre"* from varying distances in my corridor. Then all was silent again, and I no longer had a *vis-à-vis*.

For two days I had eaten nothing, and during the previous night I had slept little or not at all. After the *"Valor, hombres"* I was pretty well at the end of my tether. I thought that there was really no point in going on with all this, and wondered whether I should try that hook once more. But the idea was not very tempting. I pulled myself up by the bars of the window and in the cobwebby empty window frame discovered a splinter of glass. It was as sharp as I needed for my purpose. I was delighted with my discovery, but thought it would be better to wait until night.

The fact that I had made a decision which I regarded as final filled me with utter contentment. I became really cheerful, and the barometer rose at an astonishing rate. I called to memory, just by way of a test, the scene when the bear was led away, and the scenes in the police station. They now left me completely cold. I thought of friends and relatives, and found that I was not in the least bit moved. I was very proud of this Olympian frame of mind, and, true to the penny novelette, thought: nothing has power to move him who has done with life.

It was not until much later, in Seville, when I and a fellow prisoner, also condemned to death, were discussing the various forms of fear, that I understood the secret of this magic metamorphosis: namely, that by coming to a sham decision to take my life I had simply snatched for myself twelve untroubled hours. My state of Olympian calm was not, as I thought, the result of the decision itself, but of my having set a time limit of twelve hours. Up till now I had counted hourly on hearing the oily voice calling out my name; now, by a wishful inference, I took it for granted that the twelve hours' respite which I had given myself would be respected by the outside world. This was why I was so cheerful.

I remained so until the afternoon, and then became even more cheerful when the door opened and the kindly old warder and an assistant dragged in a straw mattress. It was a dirty old mattress, and the straw sagged and stank, but when it had been laid over the iron springs and I had stretched myself out on it, I felt in all my aching joints and limbs how marvellously comforting it was compared with the iron springs which cut into the flesh. I grunted with satisfaction; the two warders looked on and grinned while I tried the mattress. They must have seen the same thing happen many times before, and have been well aware of the enormous difference between a cell with a mattress and one without.

But a man is never satisfied; I wanted not only to have a soft, but a warm, bed to lie in. It was of course no use even dreaming of a blanket. So I tried to lie underneath the straw mattress and to use it as a blanket, but this arrangement was not satisfactory. Finally I hit upon an idea. With my splinter of glass I cut a long slit at the top end of the sacking and crept into it as I was, clothes, shoes and all, crawling into it feet foremost, and then worming my way in bit by bit until only my head peeped forth from the slit. I felt I looked like an Egyptian mummy, and I promptly fell into a blissful sleep.

But the chain of lucky events was not yet over for that day. At five o'clock we were again brought a meal, although it was not yet twenty-four hours since we had last been fed. This time we were given a tin of corned beef per head and a hunk of bread. The meals in this prison, both as regards the times at which they were served and the menus, were, to say the least of it, original.

I decided that with my treasured splinter of glass in my pocket there was no longer any reason why I should go hungry, and I ate all my bread and half the corned beef at one sitting. The only thing lacking to make my state of contentment perfect was a glass of water. But after all, you can't expect to have everything in this life. I burrowed back into the straw, scratched myself for a while, and fell asleep again.

I was awakened at about ten o'clock in the evening by a noisy clatter and trampling of feet in the corridors. I was already an expert at diagnosing the prison noises, and realized at once that a new batch of prisoners was being brought in. The doors of a number of the adjoining cells, which the oily voice had freed of their inmates that morning, were opened and closed. Then my door too was opened.

A young man came in, or rather, was hurled in. The door closed behind him immediately. He stood leaning against the wall, his head drooping forwards. His shirt presented the appearance to which I was by now accustomed; it was tattered, and spattered with blood. The lacerated head, covered with contusions and clotted blood, and the crazed look in the eyes were also by now familiar to me. New to me, however, was a certain something about the face of this man, an anatomical irregularity which I could not at first make out; his lower jaw was dislocated and pushed out of its socket; it was set unbelievably askew in his face, as though it had been put on the wrong way round. No sooner had I set eyes on him than I felt ill.

I crept out of the sacking and signed to him to sit down on the bed. He did not respond. I took him by the hand, led him two paces over to the bedstead and helped him to sit down. He continued to stare straight ahead, felt his jaw with his hand and recoiled as though he had burned himself. In my embarrassment I handed him some of the corned beef that had been left over, but he merely turned his head away. He could obviously neither eat nor speak. Perhaps not even think; but only suffer and be afraid and await the *coup de grâce*.

I sat opposite him on the ground and held his hand. After a while he withdrew it. Fumbling slowly under his belt he produced two cigarette stumps. I took them and lit one of them; it was so short that I had to bend my head back horizontally to avoid burning my nose and lips. The human wreck grinned slightly out of the corners of his eyes, and signed to me to keep the other stump, for in any case he had no more use for it. I sat opposite him for a few minutes, not daring to say anything; any word of consolation seemed to me child-ish and somehow blasphemous. Only much later, in Seville, did I learn the simple fact that in such cases the content of what one says matters little, and the tone and gesture every-thing; thus, in the prison in Seville three of us managed to lull to death in this way a little Militiaman who was more afraid even than most people of execution. He knew that we were lying, and we knew that he knew it; and yet he was comforted, and swallowed our words like a drug.

The silent *tête-à-tête* lasted only a few minutes; then my guest was taken away. He did not even turn his head when they bound his hands, on the threshold. They took him off to the left, towards the front gate. I did not hear a cell door close behind him.

Requiescat in pace.

The Olympian calm had gone, and my misery had returned. The time had come for the splinter of glass to play its part, but I was far too apathetic to do anything at all. I didn't care two straws about anything; all I wanted was to creep into my cosy sacking and seek oblivion. At this moment I was really convinced that it was only out of laziness and apathy that I did not commit suicide. Of course I was deceiving myself again. The instinct of self-preservation, shrewd and inde-structible as it is, assumes the most subtle masks. That morn-ing it had presented itself in the toga of Socrates, who, calm and collected, reaches out for the draught of hemlock. The mask had served its purpose; it had helped the mind through a crucial moment. Now it appeared in a new garb; that of St. Simeon Stylites, who squats on his column and lets the worms devour him.

That night the oily voice rang out but once. I no longer counted the names; I lay in my sack dozing, and was now just as convinced that nothing, not even the most ghastly experience, could shatter my equanimity, as I had been that morning that it was my last morning on earth. I did not creep out of my sack again until the afternoon of the next day, Friday. And then only to take the food that was brought me —a hunk of bread and a tin full of Spanish white beans. It was my first acquaintanceship with prison beans, and was hardly pleasurable.

A little later someone on my corridor began to shout for water. "*Agua, agua,*" he yelled, and drummed on the door with his fists. This seemed to me a very good idea; I was horribly thirsty after the beans, and the endless dozing on the bed had re-awakened my desire for action. I too began to drum on the door and to yell "*agua, agua.*" Somewhere or other a third prisoner joined in, and shortly afterwards the whole wing was drumming away and yelling "*agua, agua.*"

The warders arrived on the scene and burst into a flood of invective from the corridor. For a few moments there was silence; then I began to drum and yell again, and the whole wing joined in. I thought they would be sure to come and beat me up, but was not afraid; on the contrary, I only wished that at long last something would happen. I was not acting out of rage, but out of nervous excitement and craving for action. I felt refreshed after my long sleep and was in a highly fretful, wide-awake state. I found the drumming terrific fun.

After a few minutes our efforts were rewarded. The warders brought an enormous tub of water and doled it out to each of us in turn. I was given the choice of drinking either out of the greasy tin of beans or out of the ladle, and chose the latter. I drank three ladlefuls and tried to smack my lips as the "bear" had done.

The nervous craving for action persisted. I tried to think what I could do and decided to write a short story—of course only in my head, since there were neither paper nor writing materials to hand. I started off with an animal story; it was to have been a very funny story, but after the first few sentences it became unbearably sentimental, and, again in my head, I crossed the whole thing out with a large blue pencil.

Then I set about deciphering the inscriptions scratched on the cell walls. They were mostly names, with the date of arrest, and they went back as far as 1934; probably that was the last time the cell had been whitewashed. Some of the names were accompanied by a protestation of innocence; the prisoner presumably counting on the warder's reading it and passing on the information to his superiors. A great many had added to their names the initials of their party; the most frequent were the Anarchist organizations, C.N.T. and F.A.I. The Communists never wrote the initial letters of their party, but drew, instead, a hammer and sickle or a Soviet star. The initials of the Socialist Party figured only once—Social-Democrats in all countries are tidy, discreet folk who do not write on walls. More frequent was the U.G.T., the initials of the Socialist Trades Union organization.

All these inscriptions obviously dated from the period before the elections of February, 1936. Then the Left had come to power, had proclaimed a general amnesty and liberated the political prisoners; new ones came, distinguished people this time; my cell must have felt highly honoured. Perhaps Thomas Bolín had lain on this same bunk and dreamed of his pretty postcards, and of the time when he would buy a pistol to shoot the Reds. But oddly enough the inmates of the cell after this date—Monarchists, Fascists, perhaps even priests—had left no traces behind. Not once did I come upon the C.E.D.A., the initials of Gil Robles' party, nor even a simple cross. And yet the prison was as chock-full during Malaga's "red" period as it was now. Why had the reactionaries not followed the example of their predecessors? Had they less courage, or less attachment to their party, or did they simply not feel the need to immortalize themselves?

There were neither verses nor obscenities among the inscriptions; at the most one female name with a few poetic attributes scrawled beneath it. Even the popular heart pierced with a Cupid's arrow appeared only twice.

This night too passed. After the hectic mood of the last twenty-four hours with its continual ups and downs, a relatively normal state of mind set in. I reflected that four days had now passed since my arrest, and hoped that the news of it would somehow have reached England, and that there would be protests. Time would work in my favour, and a five per cent chance is always better than no chance at all.

I whiled away the sleepless parts of the night with these relatively consoling reflections.

What I did *not* know was that the court-martial in Malaga had already pronounced sentence of death on me without my being summoned before it.

The second thing that I did not know was that up to this time—Saturday, February 13th, 1937—five thousand men had been shot in Malaga since the fall of the town; six hundred from my prison alone.

IX

ROUND about midday on Saturday, the fourth day after my arrest, the door of my cell swung open again.

Outside there stood, not the now familiar figures of the warders, but two Civil Guards with rifles and fixed bayonets. "*Venga*," they said. "Come."

I still had one last cigarette in my breast pocket. I had had nothing to smoke for three days, but I had been saving this one cigarette for the time when the oily voice should call out my name. I had racked my brains to discover how to manage to preserve a decent demeanour during those last moments, and had thought that a cigarette might perhaps help.

When I saw the two men standing at the door with their bayonets, I thought that the moment had come to light up. I had just put the cigarette in my mouth when one of the Civil Guards produced a most comforting object from his pocket: a pair of steel handcuffs. I knew that they used a cord to bind the hands of those whom they were taking out to be shot; handcuffs are too precious, and removing them from a corpse is far too arduous a business. The only factory in Spain that manufactures handcuffs is in Bilbao, and Bilbao was at that time still in Government hands. There was an unlimited supply of human cattle for the slaughter on the Spanish market, but a shortage of handcuffs.

At this moment, therefore, the shining steel handcuffs were indeed the most cheering sight I could have wished for. I folded my hands piously, and the handcuffs shut to with a snap. I marvelled at the complicated and skilful mechanism of what seemed such a simple apparatus; on each of the wristlets was a little cog-wheel, to make it adjustable for any size of wrist. The elder of the Civil Guards even enquired whether the catch chafed my wrists—he asked this neither out of friendliness nor ironically, but in the businesslike tones of a tailor fitting a suit. Then we marched off down the corridors and out into the street.

Outside the prison gate stood a big lorry and an elegant little sports car. We made for the sports car. On the bonnet were four copper plaques: the first displayed the Swastika between two wings, the second the Roman fasces, the third the five black arrows of the *Falange Española*, and the fourth the coat of arms of the Bourbon dynasty.

Not even in my wildest dreams had I pictured myself going for a drive in such a stately, symbol-laden vehicle. Actually it all came to nothing; for just as we were getting in, an officer with a riding crop came rushing up to tell the Civil Guards that he was requisitioning the car, and that the lorry was good enough for us, anyway. My guards seemed put out, but did not dare to protest, and we clambered into the lorry, which was already loaded to capacity with forty prisoners and their armed escorts.

I was so exhilarated by the fresh air and the sudden change of scene after four days of solitary confinement that for the first few moments I gazed round at my fellow prisoners almost gaily; then I noticed that their hands were bound with cords. There were, besides, about ten to fifteen of them tied to each other in a group with longer cords.

We stood closely packed together. As the heavy lorry started up, we had to hold on to each other and to the Civil Guards to keep our balance. There was about the same number of Civil Guards as victims; holding their rifles in one hand, they too sought to steady themselves by putting an arm round the shoulder of a neighbour, regardless of whether he were a fellow guard or a man whom half an hour later they would be shooting, sending a bullet through his eye or his nose.

I still had my unlighted cigarette between my lips. The

Civil Guard who had put the handcuffs on me lit a cigarette for himself and was about to give me a light. I told him that it was my last cigarette and that I wanted to keep it for later on, and put it back in my pocket. He rolled me a cigarette and handed round his tobacco-pouch and paper amongst the others, both Civil Guards and prisoners. A Civil Guard helped those whose hands were bound too tightly to roll their cigarettes, holding out the finished article for them to give the final lick.

The Civil Guards looked like Andalusian farm-hands or peasants, and the prisoners too looked like Andalusian farm-hands or peasants. As they stood, clinging to each other on the bouncing lorry, one might have taken them for a charabanc party on an excursion to some green spot in the country-side. Arrived at their destination, the various rôles will be assigned: those with the ropes will stand up against a wall, the others will send hot leaden projectiles into their flesh. Naturally both groups would rather play football with each other. But that would not do; God in His wisdom has decided it must be thus and not otherwise; so the surviving half of the party will roll themselves cigarettes and climb back surlily into the lorry.

We exchanged tobacco and clung to each other when the lorry gave a lurch, and each felt the bodily warmth of his neighbour; but no one spoke.

With one exception. One of the Civil Guards, with glasses and a corporal's stripes, who was standing pressed against the barrier in a particularly cramped position, remarked with a grin to the man next to him:

"We shall be a lot more comfortable on the return journey."

But only one or two people heard, and no one answered.

A priest passed and looked at us. We too looked at him.

In the vicinity of the station the motorized tumbril drew up, and I and my two guards alighted. The first one jumped down and helped me down, since I could not use my hands, and then the second jumped down after me. The lorry drove on again. The prisoners looked after us, and I could feel envy and contempt in their gaze, and even in the eyes of their guards. We were outsiders, we had broken the bond of a common fate. We all three gazed after the lorry as it disappeared in a cloud of dust. One of my guards turned to me and went through the motions of pulling the trigger of his rifle, to dispel any lingering doubts on my part. Then he rolled cigarettes for the three of us, and we entered the station.

This Civil Guard was a lanky, loose-limbed fellow with an absurd, horse-like face. He had long, yellow, equine teeth, a flat nose, and the good-natured, stupid eyes of a cab-horse. He was called Pedro.

The other was short and sturdy, with a bronzed, vital peasant's face. He was called Luis.

While we stood about in the waiting-room, I asked the lanky Don Pedro where they were taking me. "To Seville," he said, and showed me a typed order in which it was stated that "the individual A.K. is to be brought to Seville under safe escort, and to be delivered up to the special jurisdiction of the Commander of the Southern Fighting Forces of the National Army, General González Queipo de Llano."

I had hoped that I was to be taken to Burgos or Salamanca. Of all the cities of the globe Seville was the one the name of which sounded most unfriendly to my ears. And of all the mighty ones of this world the one whom I had most cause to fear was General González Queipo de Llano.

It was scarcely six months since I had seen him face to face. The interview that he had given me and the brief but unfriendly character-sketch that I had drawn of him had already appeared, not only in the Press, but in my book in French. Queipo read French, and the book very likely lay on his desk beside my dossier. I could imagine his face while he read the chapter "Portrait of a Rebel General"; it was his own portrait and a faithful one; so much the worse for me. Now I was under his "special jurisdiction." I felt like a wanderer in the jungle who had inadvertently trodden on a tiger's tail.

We got into the train. It was an ancient train with a funny little engine and funny little carriages that looked like wooden boxes on wheels. We wormed our way into a third class compartment in which a large peasant family was already installed: father, mother, grandmother, an adolescent daughter and a baby. The family moved up closer to one another and respectfully left the two corner seats by the window to the two Civil Guards. I sat next to the lanky Don Pedro; next me was the mother with the baby, opposite me the grandmother, and next to her in the corner the adolescent daughter. She was very pretty, and she cast stealthy glances at my grimy, but still recognizably foreign, suit. I kept my hands hidden in my sleeves like a monk, so that the handcuffs were not immediately visible. The train ambled off.

The grandmother had already got into conversation with Don Pedro and Don Luis. At first they talked of the weather, then about the orange crop, then about the war. I learned that Motril had fallen since my arrest, and that the fall of Almería was hourly expected. Both the peasants and my guards avoided taking sides; they referred to Franco's army not as "*los nuestros*," "our people," but as "*los Nacionales*." The guards referred to the other side as "*los Rojos*" (the Reds) but the grandmother spoke of them as "*los Valencianos*." The family came from Antequera, the village that Pizarro used to raid for cigarettes and seed corn. In the first chaotic days after the insurrection they had fled to Malaga to take refuge with relatives and had been unable to return to their own village, which was on the other side of the Front. Then "*los Nacionales*" had taken Malaga, and now they were returning home.

Don Luis asked the husband what things had been like in
Malaga under the Reds.

The man shrugged his shoulders and said that he had never
troubled his head about politics.

The grandmother said that it was the foreigners who were
to blame for the whole tragedy; on the other side the Russians, and on this side the Germans and Italians. Then she
clapped her hand to her mouth, and enquired with a sly,
apologetic smile if I were a German airman.

No, I told her, I was an English journalist.

The daughter looked at me with interest. Don Pedro and
Don Luis grinned, but tactfully held their tongues.

The grandmother wanted to know what the King of England thought about "all this Spanish business."

I said that His Majesty had not yet come to any final conclusion, for the opinions of his advisers were somewhat contradictory.

Whereupon Don Pedro enquired, giving a crafty wink and
baring his equine teeth, whether there were also "Reds" in
England. Don Luis too winked at me and burst out into
raucous laughter. They both nudged me with their knees,
and would obviously have been offended if I had not shared
in their mirth. I did my best and joined in. It was a little
secret between the three of us.

"In the end," said the grandmother, "he'll turn out to be a
Red himself."

This remark released a flood of laughter from Don Pedro
and Don Luis, and the grandmother was very proud of her
joke.

And since we were all in such merry mood, she took down
from the rack, with the help of the mother, their basket of
provisions and a bottle of red wine.

She offered us lovely red paprika sausage and cheese and
white bread and wine. The Civil Guards accepted with alacrity; I refused. The whole family pressed me to eat. I did not

move my hands from my sleeves. It was a ghastly situation. The guards looked at each other; then Don Luis resolutely seized me by the arm and removed the handcuffs. The whole family turned to stone.

"Holy Mother of God!" cried the grandmother. She looked at me and added softly:

"Your poor mother!"

Then she passed me sausage and cheese and made the sign of the cross over me.

I began eating, and wiped the beads of sweat from my forehead. The daughter looked away, and flushed a fiery red. The baby, who had crawled on to the floor whilst the food was being unpacked, now crawled up to Don Luis and tried to play with the handcuffs.

It was about four hours before we reached Antequera. It was not on our direct route; the train made endless détours. We ate and drank a great deal, but there was no more conversation. Now and again, when the silence became painful, the taciturn peasant would say from his corner:

"Give the *Inglés* another bit of sausage," or

"Has the *Inglés* had enough wine?"

He never addressed me directly. But the mother, who was at once the friendliest and the stupidest member of the family, said, as she pressed a slice of sweet cake into my hand:

"Eat up, Señor. Who knows how much longer you'll be able to eat!"

Whereat Don Pedro remarked jokingly:

"He's going to be shot to-morrow."

But his joke was coldly received, and Don Pedro grew quite embarrassed, obviously feeling that he had committed a *faux pas.*

At one of the small stations he got out to get some water, giving me his rifle and the handcuffs to hold in the meantime. He did this as though absent-mindedly, in his hurry, but I had a feeling that he was doing it on purpose, to atone for his previous lapse. He brought back some tobacco and a packet of ten cigarettes at 10 centimos, which he presented to me. I handed them round and everyone took one out of politeness, although they were much inferior to the rolled ones. In Antequera the family got out with a great deal of bustle and fuss. The grandmother once more made the sign of the cross over me; the peasant, without a word, handed me an orange; the daughter blushed again and avoided looking at me. Then the train went on.

It was late afternoon by now, and we all three stretched ourselves out on the seat and fell asleep.

A few stations later more passengers got in, among them a young man and a somewhat corpulent gentleman of the upper classes. They too began a conversation, and in order to avoid fresh complications I myself explained at once that I was a prisoner, although the handcuffs had not been put on me again. The representative of the upper classes thereupon moved into the furthest corner of the carriage and kept glancing at me as though I were a leper. The young man, who, like the peasant and everyone else on the train, was wearing the Nationalist cockade in his buttonhole, offered me a cigarette, and, noticing that I had no coat and was shivering, his rug. He told me that he was going to Seville because he had been requested to report as a recruit to the Phalanx. I asked him why, then, he gave "an enemy" his rug. He shrugged his shoulders and winked ever so slightly. I do not know whether Queipo de Llano will be exactly pleased with this Phalangist; or with some thousands like him.

The handcuffs were not put on me again until we reached Seville.

It was quite late at night by then. Don Pedro and Don Luis were once more full of official solemnity, and we marched in single file into the *gendarmerie* on the station.

There a discussion took place as to what was to be done with me at this late hour—it was a quarter past twelve. There was no official car available, and the trams were no longer running. Don Luis suggested that they should take me to the Phalangist barracks just for the night. This was exactly what I had been dreading. I asked Don Pedro whether they could not take me to the prison instead. He grinned and said: "I suppose you don't like the idea of going to the Phalanx?" I said that I didn't. They both grinned and whispered together for a while, and then Don Pedro said they would telephone to General Staff Headquarters, for that was, after all, the authority to deal with my case. They asked an official for the telephone book; he replied that there wasn't one, but that all official numbers were written up on the wall in the telephone booth. So we went into the booth.

The walls were covered with numbers written in pencil. "Italian Base Headquarters, Number So-and-so," I read. "Italian Infantry Barracks, Number So-and-so." "Italian Infantry Barracks No. 2, Number So-and-so." "Italian Commissariat, Number So-and-so."

The tourist traffic in the town of Seville had obviously increased since my last visit.

At last our joint efforts resulted in our finding the number of the General Staff of the Southern Forces.

Don Luis telephoned, and half an hour later a car came to the station to fetch us.

We drove through the streets of Seville, past the Hotel Madrid, where I had once stayed, past the Hotel Cristina, where I had met Strindberg and the German pilots, past the Phalangist barracks, where I had seen the blood-bespattered prisoners from the Rio Tinto mines being marched in, to the familiar residence of the "radio General." It was an eerie drive, worse than the drive to the Malaga prison when I had imagined that I was being taken to the cemetery. Don Pedro and Don Luis were silent, and I longed for them never to leave me.

The corridors of Staff Headquarters were nocturnally bleak

and deserted. Only in a few rooms were people still working; we were sent from one to another, and no one knew what to do with us. Finally we landed up somewhere in the decoding department. There we found a pleasant official who said we might all three sleep on the floor. Don Luis had already squatted on the floor to take off his boots when an officer appeared and ordered us out. He said I had no business to be in the decoding department; the place for me was the police station. So we wandered off to the police station.

Don Pedro and Don Luis were tired out and in a bad temper; I was obviously a nuisance to them, and they would much rather have let me go. But that would never have done; and so at length we ended up in the police station.

We found ourselves in a smelly office, where a surly fellow noted down particulars of my case, and took my finger prints. Then he called two sergeants. They stood to attention at their Chief's table—two gorillas. They saluted, and one of them asked in an official tone:

"Una *flagelación?*"

Flagelación is the term used for the first beating to which an arrested man is subjected in Spanish police stations. It is an illegal but official practice carried out in most countries of Europe. In France it is called *passer à tabac*, and in Germany *die erste Abreibung*.

Don Luis bent assiduously over to the Chief and whispered a few words in his ear. All I could catch was: "*Inglés—periodista*." Whereupon the *flagelación* was dispensed with.

I was greatly relieved, and the two gorillas, balked of their prey, led me into a kind of cage with an iron grille. Don Luis and Don Pedro, a few minutes later, when their official papers had been examined and stamped, came past the cage. I called out to them and thanked them for being so nice to me on the journey. They grew very embarrassed, and shook hands with me in turn through the grille. The gorillas opened their eyes wide, and my two friends departed.

They were not exceptions; they were two out of twenty-five million for the most part kindly Spaniards. Had they been given orders, before we made friends on the journey, to strike me dead or to shoot me, they would have done so with complete sang-froid. Had they been fellow prisoners, they would have shared their last cigarette with me. Had I, on the other hand, made the railway journey with the two unfriendly gorillas, we would most likely have parted with the same cordial feelings.

I looked at the gorillas and the gorillas looked at me, and I wondered what they would have done to me had the *flagelación* not been called off. As it happened to be called off, they gave me cigarettes with a sheepish grin. I grinned back and thought how ridiculous it is that we place so much importance on the personal character of a man; how little depends on what a man is, and how much on the function which society has given him to fulfil; and how limited a field is left to him in which to develop his natural propensities. What difference did it make whether Don Luis and Don Pedro and the gendarmes on the tumbril were endowed with a musical ear or not, whether they preferred cats or dogs, and whether they were good or bad? Suddenly I seemed to understand why the Anarchist doctrine is so popular in Spain. To the Anarchists the problem of the human race is as simple as cracking nuts: just smash the hard shell of social institutions and savour the delicious kernel. A fascinating theory; but it seemed to me rather doubtful whether trees would ever bear nuts without shells.

One is never so curious about the future of humanity as when one is locked up in an iron cage, guarded by two gorillas, and would rather think of anything but one's own future. I believe that the only consolation you could give to a condemned man on his way to the electric chair would be to tell

him that a comet was on the way which would destroy the
world the very next day.

Round about two or three o'clock in the morning a car arrived and transported me, under the escort of the two gorillas,
right across the sleeping city, across the Guadalquivir bridge
and down deserted avenues, to the distant prison of Seville.

X

THE sight of the prison building looming up out of the darkness was as comforting to me as had been the sight of the handcuffs fifteen hours earlier. I knew by this time that prisoners were only beaten and maltreated at police stations, Phalangist headquarters and barracks, but not in prison. There were two roads leading out of prison: to freedom or the firing squad. But so long as one was in prison itself, one was safe.

I surveyed the massive building with feelings of grateful affection. The rottenness of a civilization reveals itself in curious symptoms; in the fact, for example, that the stone walls of prisons no longer serve to protect society from the prisoner, but the prisoner from society.

The prison of Seville had been built in the first few years after the Spanish revolution, in 1931 or 1932. The young and ambitious Republic wished to emulate, and, if possible, to excel, the civilized West in everything. Among its finest achievements must be counted reforms in the sphere of penology, up till that time on a medieval level in Spain. The "model prisons" which were built in Madrid, Barcelona and Seville are, in fact, the best and most up-to-date prisons in Europe.

We crossed the lovely garden in front of the main gate, rang—here too there was a night bell—and the gate was opened.

Three long corridors radiated out from the entrance hall; one leading straight on, the others to the right and to the left. The corridors were flanked by long, monotonous rows of cell doors, two tiers of them on either side. The cells on the upper floor opened on to narrow steel galleries which were reached by steel staircases. Each cell door bore a number and a name plate, and was fitted with a spy-hole. Everything that met the eye was of steel and concrete; everything looked fantastically standardized, symmetrical, machine-like. Gazing at this framework of steel one might have imagined oneself in the engine-room of a warship.

In the middle of the hall, facing the entrance, was a kind of glass case: the office. For the third time I went through the procedure of having my particulars noted, my person searched and my finger prints taken. The demeanour of the officials made one feel one was not in a prison, but in an income-tax office, in the midst of a group of polite and slightly bored clerks.

The gorillas took their departure. A young, friendly and taciturn warder took charge of me and led me down the central corridor. The first cell to the right which we passed—Cell No. 44—bore the name Caballero.

Largo Caballero was at that time Prime Minister of the Government in Valencia. I knew that his son, whom the insurrection had taken by surprise in Seville, was being held as a hostage by the rebels. Some days before I had left Paris the newspapers had reported that he had been executed. So this news was false; for here on Cell No. 44 was the visiting card of Caballero Junior. This seemed to me very gratifying, and I had a positive urge to knock on his door and call out: "Doctor Livingstone, I presume?"

We passed cells Nos. 43 and 42; they bore Spanish names. At Cell No. 41 we stopped, and the warder unlocked the door. This, then, was my new home.

It was, if the adjective is in place here, a room of pleasant, square proportions. The first thing that struck me was the big window opposite the door. It was let into a kind of alcove in the wall and began at the level of the head, so that by supporting one's elbows on the slant of the wall one could look out quite comfortably. The window gave on to the patio, a very large and dusty prison courtyard. It was protected by a solid iron grille, and outside the grille was fixed fine wire netting, rather like a steel mosquito net.

Against the wall to the right was the iron bedstead, which could be folded back against the wall to allow more room for pacing up and down; opposite it was a steel table with a chair welded to it, also collapsible. At the foot of the bed was a large wash-basin with running water; opposite it the W.C.

The warder tested the straw mattress, to which was attached a linen tab with a date stamped on it, obviously to show when the straw had last been changed and the mattress cleaned. He brought in a good woollen blanket and said that he would change both mattress and blanket for clean ones next morning. Then he wished me good night and carefully locked the door from outside.

After Malaga it seemed to me that I was in a luxury hotel.

I went to the window and looked out; it was a starry night, and the courtyard was still and peaceful. Opposite my window, along the wall at the further end of the court, a guard patrolled up and down with fixed bayonet, smoking a cigarette. With a small effort of imagination one might have fancied that he was promenading out there not in order to guard us but to protect us.

It was half-past two. I lay down on the straw mattress, revelled in the wonderful luxury of possessing a blanket, and fell contentedly asleep.

I was awakened by a bugle-blast; it was a quarter to seven in the morning. I assumed that it was the signal to get up, but feigned deafness and went on sleeping. The next time I woke up it was nine o'clock, and the sound of shouts and clattering feet came in through the window. I looked out; the courtyard was full of prisoners, who, with true Spanish fervour, were engaged in a football match, some as players, some as spectators.

There may have been three to four hundred men in the

courtyard. They were not in uniform, and they were moving about freely in the great quadrangle, which was about a hundred yards by sixty. It was only some time later that I picked out a uniformed warder among them, who, a revolver in his belt and a rubber truncheon in his hand, patrolled up and down, exchanging a word here and there with the prisoners, or even walking about in conversation with one of them. The prisoners all wore civilian clothes and yet created a fairly uniform impression, for the overwhelming majority of them appeared to be young Andalusian peasants and wore the same kind of clothes; bluish-green faded linen shirts and jackets. A uniform effect was created, moreover, by their unshaven state, their bare heads and bronzed faces. The young lads who were playing football chased across the courtyard after the ball, which was made of rags bound together with string. Another group was engaged in a game of leap-frog along the opposite wall. When, under the force of the impact, one of the "frogs" fell flat on his stomach together with the jumper, there were roars of laughter. The warder stood by and joined in the fun. The more sedate elders were shying little pebbles at a target; others were sitting in the narrow strip of shade, reading.

And all this festive activity was going on just outside my window, which was on a level with the ground. After the bloody nightmare of Malaga it all seemed like a dream. For five days I had crouched in my isolation cell, which stank of blood and excrement, had not seen a single human countenance except that of the warder, had not heard a single human sound except the oily voice of the invisible herald of death. The hullabaloo in the courtyard, the change of scene, the plenitude of faces and human destinies that offered itself to the view, positively dazzled and intoxicated me. I leaned on my elbows in the alcove, waved and called out to the courtyard. At first the fact that no one heard me or seemed to want to hear me did not worry me. Nor for the moment did it strike me that no one passed directly by my window; indeed, that an empty space several feet wide was left alongside the wall separating me from the courtyard.

There was a rattling at the lock of my door. I turned away from the window to see who was coming; for the first time since my arrest I heard the cell door opening without my heart's being constricted with fear. It was the warder who had taken charge of me in the night; he looked round the cell and began to curse me for not having got up at the first bugle-blast and washed the floor.

He roared until the walls shook, but it was nothing to worry about. He swore at me as a corporal swears at a recruit, and involuntarily I answered like a raw recruit who has just arrived in barracks and doesn't yet know the routine. He quickly calmed down and explained to me that I must first sweep the flagstones with a broom and then scour them with a pail and floor-cloth.

I took the broom and began to sweep, assuming an air of distinguished incompetence, until the warder had had enough of it and said he would call the orderly to show me how to set about things. Opening the door he called out into the corridor:

"*Angel, Angelito!*"

The "angelkin" thus evoked came shuffling up and set about sweeping the floor with ape-like agility. He had the face of an old woman; his skin was like crinkled parchment and his figure that of a twelve-year-old child. He never once looked either me or the warder in the face, and as he crept about the cell on all fours, his eyes darted about swiftly, like the eyes of a shrew. In less than two minutes the cell had been swept, swilled with water and apparently thoroughly scoured. It was positively a star turn. When warder and angelkin had departed and the floor began to dry I could see that the flags were as dirty as before.

Shortly afterwards breakfast arrived: a tin bowl full of appetizing coffee, ladled out of a huge tub, and a white roll. It was Angelito who brought the breakfast round. He seemed to be maid-of-all-work here. I asked him to report that I should like to be shaved, so as not to look like a bandit at my trial; for I was expecting hourly to be at length brought to trial. But Angelito vouchsafed no reply and slammed the door in my face.

I once more took up my observation post at the window and watched the activities in the courtyard until midday. Bit by bit I began to pick out single individuals from the anonymous crowd. An old man was the first to rivet my attention; he must have been over seventy; he walked with a slight stoop and wore a warm woolly ulster. He immediately won my sympathy. Then there were a few boys of no more than thirteen or fourteen. I thought they must be hostages from Red families. Three or four strikingly elegantly dressed men with immaculate creases in their trousers and brightly polished shoes paced up and down apart from the others, with portentous expressions. I christened them "the dandies" and wondered what could have brought them here.

I wondered, too, whether all these men were political prisoners or criminals. Their faces seemed to suggest the former; but I noticed that about nine or ten of them were wearing a stripe in the Bourbon colours on their shirts, and that these were by no means shunned by the rest. This did not fit in with my ideas as to the atmosphere amongst political prisoners.

Everyone in the courtyard was smoking, and tobacco and cigarette papers were being handed round freely. After having been treated to cigarettes on the journey, I found my renewed abstinence particularly hard. I bored a tiny hole with my index finger in the wire mosquito net in front of my window—large enough for a cigarette to be pushed through. It was quite easy; I only had to force the wires apart a little. I knew that the inside of my cell must appear dark from the courtyard and so I pressed my face against the iron bars and began to make signs to those outside that I wanted something to smoke.

At first I had a feeling that it was only by chance that no one looked in my direction. I began to call out, but there was such a din in the quadrangle that I found it difficult to make myself heard; for after all I did not want to shout. All the same, those nearest to me must have heard. But no one responded.

To be ignored in this way gave me a very uncomfortable feeling. Now I noticed, too, that some of the prisoners could perfectly well hear and see my signals as they passed, but quickly averted their heads. And once more it occurred to me that no one came within ten paces of that part of the wall where my cell was.

At last I saw one of the peasant lads in a linen packet drawing the attention of some of the others to my window. But he did so very discreetly. Three or four of his companions looked stealthily in my direction. I gesticulated more vehemently and signed to them to pass a cigarette through to me. They seemed embarrassed and at a loss to know what to do, and looked round anxiously at the warder, although he was at the further end of the courtyard. Then one of them quickly put a finger to his lips and shrugged his shoulders, and the group hurried off.

It takes some time to make out details in the chaotic bustle and stir of a courtyard containing three or four hundred people. Thus it was not until now that I noticed that a faded and scarcely visible white line, rather like the marking on a neglected tennis court, was drawn parallel to my wall. The line began at the end of my row of cells, in front of No. 44, the cell containing Caballero, ran past my window, and ended some cells further to the left, as far as I could tell in front of Cell No. 36. Further down, from No. 35 downwards, the prisoners approached the wall quite freely and spoke to the inmates of the cells through the windows. But from Nos. 36

to 44 there was a no-man's land ten yards wide between the wall and the white line. The cells opposite this line, which included mine, were obviously taboo.

And now suddenly I realized that the men in the courtyard were afraid. Afraid of being watched. They obviously knew that every one of their movements was being spied upon. They could see what I could not see; that from the upper storey windows watchful glances were cast at the courtyard below. There must be something peculiar and uncanny behind all this demonstrative gaiety.

And now I couldn't understand what was happening. What ghostly carnival was this? Were all these men, playing leap-frog and football and strolling about in the bright sunshine of the patio, were they only waiting for the second cock-crow —or waiting for an oily voice to call out their names?

Why had I been put into a taboo cell? Why was I not allowed to join the others in the court and why were the prisoners in the court so afraid of looking in my direction? Was it indeed fear—or was it the embarrassment with which the healthy avert their gaze from the gravely ill, who bear the stamp of death on their brows?

And now at last I admitted to myself what had gradually been dawning on me from the start. I had been put in one of the condemned cells.

The midday meal arrived: bean soup cooked in oil and a hunk of white bread. The soup was served in the same bowl out of which I had drunk my breakfast coffee and had slaked my thirst with water. Once more it was Angelito who brought me my food, this time, however, accompanied by a warder. The warder had a red full-moon face, and spoke a little French. He was glad to be able to air his knowledge to a foreigner, and listened patiently while I enumerated my requests: I wanted to be shaved, I wanted a bit of soap, a comb and a towel; I wanted pencil and paper in order to write to the

British Consul; I wanted a book to read from the prison library, and some newspapers; I wanted to be allowed out into the courtyard like the other prisoners; I wanted back the money that had been confiscated from me to buy cigarettes and a change of linen.

He listened to all this attentively, and nodded after each sentence as though to indicate that he considered my wishes quite proper and reasonable.

I said that he had better write them down so as not to forget anything.

He replied that he never forgot anything, for he had a very good memory, and tapped his forehead to emphasize this. Then he said that he would come back in a moment, and disappeared. I waited for him to return, and he did in fact return —exactly a fortnight later, when his turn of duty brought him to my cell again. He was just as friendly, talked away just as assiduously as the first time, and listened just as patiently while I enumerated exactly the same requests that I had repeated three times a day for a fortnight to his fellow warders —and with just as little success.

The midday meal had arrived shortly before one; at one the prisoners were brought back into their cells from the courtyard. The siesta in Spain lasts from one to three; in offices, factories, at the front and in prison.

For about a quarter of an hour the great quadrangle lay empty and deserted.

Then in the wall opposite my cell the door was opened and two prisoners were let out into the courtyard.

They were both very tidily and neatly dressed. They immediately began to march up and down at a rapid pace. One had a slightly swaying, dandified gait, and something definitely daring and enterprising about him. I christened him "Lord Byron." His friend was quieter and more self-contained; his cheeks were extraordinarily hollow, and he gave one the impression of being a consumptive.

They walked up and down the whole length of the court-yard without stopping for two hours, until the stroke of three. Then a warder took them back into the prison. Ten minutes later the crowd of the morning was once more let out into the courtyard.

I passed the afternoon spying out of my alcove window, but I no longer tried to signal or to get into touch with the throng outside. I was glad enough for no one to look in the direction of my window, glad to take part in the brilliant life outside as a silent and invisible onlooker.

Shortly before seven the evening meal was brought: lentil soup cooked in oil and a hunk of bread.

The prisoners were fed outside.

Shortly before eight they were brought back into the building. The empty courtyard was soon flooded with darkness.

At nine a bugle was sounded. At ten the Spanish last post, a very sentimental and melancholy melody, was sounded.

In the cell above me someone took his shoes off and let them fall with a clatter on to the stone floor.

Then the noises died down and the deaf silence of the prison filled every crack and cranny as though with cotton wool.

But the electric light in my cell burned the whole night long.

XI

DURING this second night in Seville I repeatedly started up out of my dreams, thinking I could hear noises and the oily voice of the Malaga prison. But there was utter silence. It was good to have a light burning, even though the bulb in the ceiling shone straight into my eyes.

Electric light scares away nocturnal spectres. Still drowsy from my nightmare, I told myself that this was a real prison and not a slaughter-house like the place in Malaga; after seven months of Civil War conditions had no doubt become normal again. Here there were certainly no more executions. True, I had been put in a condemned cell, but that probably meant nothing at all. The day here had its prescribed course, life was ordered, there were bugle-blasts, even the mattresses bore tabs stamped with the date. Incidentally it occurred to me that, despite the warder's promise, my mattress and blanket had not been changed. This annoyed me; and then I felt glad at being able to get annoyed again about trifles. Lord, I begged, go on giving me my little daily vexations. Permit me, O Lord, to continue to be discontented with this existence, to curse my work, not to answer my letters, and to be a trial to my friends. Am I to swear to grow better if Thou lettest this cup pass from me? We both of us know, Lord, Thou and I, that such extorted oaths are never kept. Do not blackmail me, Lord God, and do not try to make a saint of me. Amen. Then the bugle-blast woke me up.

This time I got up at once, washed and tidied myself as well as I could without soap and comb, and cleaned out the cell; I was full of good resolutions to adapt myself to the new order of things. A tune from a German film haunted me: "A new life is just beginning." It was a stupid film which I had seen a year previously and never given a thought to again. In the night the tune had buzzed in my ear like a tiresome fly, and I couldn't get rid of it. "A new life is just beginning."

At eight the prisoners came out into the courtyard again, and I took up my observation post. By now I seemed to myself to be like some Parisian *petit-bourgeois* who, in shirtsleeves and with pipe in mouth, leans out of the window to watch the stir and bustle of the market.

Later on I busied myself with the equation of a hyperbola again. The walls of this cell were beautifully white and unsullied, and provided an extensive surface upon which to write. A piece of wire from my bedstead once more served me for pencil.

I also began to scrawl my diary on the wall, but I stuck over it. As long as I was thinking them out, my sentences seemed quite sensible, but no sooner had I begun to scribble them down than I fell as though bewitched into the sentimental penny novelette style. At midday there were beans in oil again. I wondered whether they cooked once for the whole week.

Punctually at one Byron and the consumptive once more appeared in the courtyard, to disappear punctually again at three. I racked my brains wondering what crime they could have committed not to be allowed out with the rest of the prisoners; I decided they must be in a kind of intermediate stage between the solitary confinement in which I was kept and the comparative freedom of the others.

That afternoon a minor catastrophe befell me; my watch stopped. It gave me an awful fright. I thought to myself that if there were no longer any ladder-rungs of hours and minutes on which to cling, I should be bound to sink beyond hope of salvation into the stupefying sameness of time. But I poked about among the wheels with my iron all-purpose gadget until it went again.

The rest of the afternoon was spent in mathematics, reciting poetry and the Trojan war.

Then once more there was lentil soup and the last post.

And once more an electrically lighted night set in.

The next day was Tuesday, February 16th. I had already scratched strokes on the wall so as not to lose count of time according to conventional reckoning. The first thing that the morning bugle-blast impressed on my consciousness was that it was a week to-day since my arrest. I thought to myself that dates were kept in prison in very much the same way as in the case of newly-born infants; first of all the weeks were celebrated, then the months, then the years.

To-day it was the turn of Bible history, then French literature. But these subjects had little attraction for me. I realized with horror that my education consisted chiefly of lacunæ, and that the moths had devoured it like old academic robes. I just could not concentrate, or lose myself in a day-dream. The footballers in the courtyard observed no offside rules; they irritated and bored me. The helm of my thoughts no longer responded to my touch; I turned the wheel in vain; it ran free. I killed time by killing flies. In the midst of this occupation I had an attack of Thou-Shalt-Not-Kill feelings; it was like a slight touch of religious mania. All attempts at orderly thinking hurt me physically, and I had a feeling that all the association-centres of my brain were inflamed.

The barometer fell and fell. "Change" had long since been passed, the needle had long since travelled through "storm, wind, and rain"; all that was left was dense gloomy fog and depression.

And, to crown all, another sleepless night, which, without transition, dragged in its wake the next day, the eighth, with its repetition of bugle-calls, oily beans, of still more pitiable and unsuccessful attempts to think, to pull oneself together, to be a thinking being and not a pitiful rag.

On the afternoon of this eighth day I had a feeling that it

was impossible to sink any lower. I thought, as one does in one's naïveté, that the stage would soon be reached when madness would set in. Then it occurred to me that Dante had sat chained to a bench in a dark dungeon for four years, unable either to pace to and fro or lie down. For four years, that is, one thousand five hundred days. And *he* had not gone mad.

I tried to keep this example before my eyes; and the fate of Roman slaves and prisoners chained to the galleys; and to take heart from the consoling thought of the relatively "lesser evil." But that is the tritest of consolations. To tell a man who has had a foot amputated that there are others who have had both feet amputated is not to console him but to jeer at him. There is a degree of misery where all quantitative comparisons cease to mean anything.

Moreover, it occurred to me, an ordinary "lifer" has one advantage; at least he knows that he is not going to be hanged, and so adapts himself. A life sentence is after all a life sentence, and means at least security and the cessation of fear. One gets used to everything, runs an old saying. Uncertainty is almost as bad as death, says another.

These were monotonous reflections and they went round in my head like a mill-wheel; a threepenny mill-wheel of the cheapest and commonest wood.

Moreover, I had no need to envy the "lifers" much longer. Three days later I received the first official communication from the authorities. I had been condemned to death, but this sentence might be commuted to life-long imprisonment.

In the midst of all this misery a Messiah appeared at half-past four, in the person of the barber.

During these first few days I was continually being surprised by my own psychological reactions. The unusual conditions in which I was living produced unusual reactions; the whole machinery of my mind functioned according to new laws, completely strange to me. I felt like a driver who thinks he knows his car inside out and then suddenly realizes that it responds to pressure on the accelerator with a swerve and to the application of the brakes by looping the loop. The appearance of the barber, for example, precipitated such an earthquake in my feelings that I literally had to clutch on to the water-tap so as not to fall down. I felt, *horribile dictu,* my eyes grow moist. The barber was reflected through the prisms of the tear-drops in my eyes in all the colours of the rainbow, in a shimmering halo. He was the redeemer who was to save me from every ill. He had come, and all was well again, and the granite blocks of my fears and misery floated off gracefully into the air as though they had been filled with gas.

In the physics of madness a pebble can not only set an avalanche in motion but can also stop it. The avalanche of my despair melted away into the white flakes of the soft foam with which the barber lathered my cheeks. Ring the bells, ring the bells, I am being shaved; I am back on earth again.

Whilst I was being shaved Don Antonio, the nice warder who had been on duty in the patio the day before, stood by supervising the ceremonial.

He was the first warder to enter into a real conversation with me; for since I was *incomunicado* it was forbidden to talk to me, and up till now the warders had confined themselves to a few monosyllabic remarks when bringing me my food. The cell was like a vault enclosed in three-fold armourplating; the three-fold wall of silence, loneliness and fear.

Oh, the immense solace of simple human friendliness! The barber soaped away, Don Antonio sat down and smoked on the bed, and the three-fold wall collapsed like the walls of Jericho. The barber asked me whether the razor scratched. I said that it was a very fine razor. Don Antonio asked me whether I wished to smoke. I said that I would very much like to smoke. The barber shaved away. Don Antonio rolled me a cigarette and lit it for me. Oh, Susanna, oh, Susanna, life is lovely after all!

Every heavy smoker knows that the first cigarette after

several days of abstinence produces a feeling of slight tipsiness. I smoked almost without stopping, taking deep, thirsty puffs, and the cell began to rock slightly.

A few minutes later, when the barber had begun to cut my hair, I had gained control of myself sufficiently to enter into a sensible conversation with Don Antonio. I learned that the inmates of the big patio were actually all political prisoners; partly war prisoners, partly Republicans, Socialists, Communists and Anarchists from Seville and the surrounding villages.

In addition there were a number of Phalangists and Legionaries from Franco's army who had been imprisoned on account of desertion or breaches of discipline. There were even two Moors; I had heard one the evening before gurgling melancholy Arabian songs.

Don Antonio refused to say a word about the lengths of the sentences or discuss the question of the prisoners' trials; but he shrugged his shoulders expressively and I gained the impression that the majority of the prisoners, particularly the peasants, who were suspect because of their views, had not been brought to trial at all.

A few prisoners also had been brought over from Malaga a week previously. But they were no longer there. I asked with understandable interest what had become of them. "*Se marcharon*" (they have gone), said Don Antonio, with another shrug of the shoulders, and he refused to say anything more on this point.

I asked whether there were any criminals in the prison.

"A few," said Don Antonio. "They exercise over there in the 'beautiful patio'." The "beautiful patio" was in the other wing; it was smaller, and there were flowers, trees and benches in it. Formerly—by formerly Don Antonio always meant the time of the Republic—formerly the beautiful patio had been for political prisoners, and the big or ordinary one for criminals. Now things had been reversed.

The riddle of the national cockade worn by the political

prisoners was also cleared up. Cockades were sewn on to the shirts of those prisoners who performed some particular function, like Angelito, the orderly, the librarian, etc. I asked what sort of curious bird Angelito was. Don Antonio said he was a petty criminal; he had beaten his mother-in-law with a leather strap; luckily she had not died, but had only been paralysed on one side.

Finally I asked Don Antonio what he thought of my own personal prospects. But this was the third point on which Don Antonio refused to be drawn.

On parting I enumerated my usual list of requests, from money to pencil, from Consul to soap. He promised, as all the other warders had promised, to see to everything promptly; the result was exactly the same as in the case of all the others. This combination of utter good nature and utter unreliability in the Spaniards again and again had the effect on me of some natural phenomenon. "*Mañana, mañana*" (to-morrow, to-morrow) they said, with the most enchanting smile, or "*ahora, ahora*" (in a moment, in a moment). Both these expressions are used synonymously, and mean, according to the context: "Some time; perhaps; we must hope for the best; Allah is great; there's no need to despair."

On departing, Don Antonio gave me ten cigarettes and the barber the broken half of an old greasy comb and a bit of soap. These were wonderful presents. My standard of life was beginning to rise perceptibly.

On the afternoon of this Wednesday and the morning of the Thursday that followed it the fine weather persisted. I amused myself by inventing a peripatetic dialogue between Karl Marx and Sigmund Freud on the causes of the Great War. Both wore white togas, spoke in the manner of the disciples of Socrates, and flapped their white drapery excitedly in the midst of a group of admiring young men.

At midday there was potato soup for the first time, with so

much red pepper in it that the oil gleamed a bright scarlet. My standard of life was unmistakably rising, and, following the Coué system, I scratched on the wall: "Every day, in every way, things are getting better and better."

That afternoon, however, it rained, and the courtyard remained empty. I missed the usual hubbub and I carried on a desperate windmill struggle against a fresh wave of melancholy. But in the evening there was a sensation. Don Antonio was on duty again, and he asked me, while Angelito was ladling out the lentil soup into my bowl what English prisons were like. I said hastily that I would gladly tell him everything about them if he would stay a while and not bang the door in my face this time. I was avid of every word I was permitted to exchange with a fellow human being. Don Antonio stood leaning against the door somewhat hesitatingly. He said that he had wondered for a long time whether there were baths in every cell in English prisons. I said there were no baths, but hot and cold showers and soap *ad lib*. Don Antonio said that when the war was over he was going to England to study prison conditions there. I said that he must come and stay with me so that I might have an opportunity of returning his hospitality. He laughed and went off. I begged him to stay a while, but once more he banged the door in my face.

But those few trifling words had the effect of a stimulating drug, the effect of which lasted several hours.

And then the last post sounded again, and it was time to take off one's shoes, lie down fully dressed on the bed and, the electric light burning above one's head, to play "catch-as-catch-can" with sleep, which is, after all, one way of passing the time.

And I blessed the wisdom of the Lord, who has so ordered the world that the day has only twenty-four hours and not twenty-five or thirty.

XII

FRIDAY, February 19th, began, like all other days, with my scratching a fresh mark on my wall calendar. I discovered that a week had gone by since I had been brought to Seville—another "celebration day." Three more days, and I should be able to celebrate the fourteenth day since my arrest. The little marks on the wall displayed a dangerous tendency to increase by·division like bacilli on a dung-heap. And still I had not been brought up for trial, had not even been informed officially of the reason for my arrest. Bolín, who had arrested me, had presumably long since returned to the Salamanca headquarters, and Queipo de Llano, to whose paternal care he had handed me over, did not seem to be taking an exactly lively interest in me.

I worked out the most varying theories as to what was going on behind the scenes. The most likely explanation seemed to be that Queipo had sent for my dossier and that some authority or other was at the moment too busy to translate my book and my articles, amongst them my interview with Queipo himself, which were to constitute the main body of the evidence against me. If this were the case, then I had no cause to rejoice at the time thus gained.

On the other hand I was convinced that protests must by now have been got going on my behalf. The *News Chronicle* would protest, the journalists' associations would protest, and quite a nice little scandal would be raised. But what did Franco care about protests? Not a brass farthing. It had become a tradition during the last few years that dictators acted and democracies protested, a division of labour which seemed to please everybody.

At five o'clock in the afternoon, however, the unfriendly powers in whose hands my fate lay sent their first deputation to me. They employed, oddly enough, as official emissary, not a military examiner or any other dignitary of that kind, but a smiling young lady. She wore a well-fitting Phalangist uniform, was called Helena, like the goddess who kindled the Trojan war, and acted on the side as correspondent of the American Hearst Press.

She arrived in the company of two equally elegant young officers.

It was, as I have said, on the stroke of five that the key rattled in the lock, the door swung open and the three of them strode into my cell. They greeted me with extreme politeness and then looked round, somewhat at a loss, for something to sit upon.

The sudden opening of his cell door at a time other than the regular feeding time is always a shock to a prisoner. For the first few moments I was thrown into such confusion by the sight of the three uniformed figures that I murmured some idiotic kind of apology at being unable to offer the young lady anything better to sit on than my iron bedstead. But she only smiled—a rather charming smile it seemed to me —and asked if my name was Koestler, and whether I spoke English. To both questions I replied in the affirmative.

Then she asked me whether I was a Communist. To this I had to reply in the negative.

"But you are a Red, aren't you?"

I said that I was in sympathy with the Valencia Government, but did not belong to any party.

The young lady asked me whether I was aware what would be the consequence of my activities.

I said that I was not.

"Well," she said, "it means death."

She spoke with an American twang, drawling out the vowel

sound in "death" so that it sounded like "dea-ea-h-th," and watched the effect.

I asked why.

Because, she said, I was supposed to be a spy.

I said that I was not, and that I had never heard of a spy who signed articles and a book attacking one side in a war and then afterwards went into the territory of that side with his passport in his pocket.

She said that the authorities would investigate that point, but that in the meantime General Franco had been asked by the *News Chronicle* and by Mr. Hearst of New York to spare my life; that she happened to be the correspondent of the Hearst Press in Spain, and that General Franco had said that I would be condemned to death, but that he might possibly grant a commutation of my sentence.

I asked her what exactly she meant by a commutation.

"Well, life-long imprisonment. But there is always hope of an amnesty, you know," she said, with her charming smile.

A perfect cyclone of thoughts rushed through my head. First of all I had had a set of dirty postcards to thank for my life, and now here was Randolph Hearst himself as my second saviour—my guardian angels seemed to be a somewhat poor lot. And then, what was the significance of that fateful phrase, "*might possibly* grant a commutation"?

But I had not much time for reflection. The young lady on my bed asked me in charming conversational tones if I would like to make a statement to her paper with regard to my feelings towards General Franco.

I was pretty bewildered by all this, but not so bewildered as not to perceive the fateful connection between this question and that "might possibly" of General Franco's. This was something like a Biblical temptation, although Satan was presenting himself in the smiling mask of a young woman journalist; and at that moment—after all those days of waiting for torture and death—I had not the moral strength to resist.

So I said that although I did not know Franco personally I had a feeling that he must be a man of humanitarian outlook whom I could trust implicitly. The young lady wrote this down, seemingly very pleased, and asked me to sign it.

I took the pen, and then I realized that I was about to sign my own moral death sentence, and that this sentence no one could commute. So I crossed out what she had written and dictated another statement, which ran:

"I do not know General Franco personally, nor he me; and so, if he grants me a commutation of my sentence I can only suppose that it is mainly from political considerations.

"Nevertheless, I could not but be personally grateful to him, just as any man is grateful to another who saves his life. But I believe in the Socialist conception of the future of humanity, and shall never cease to believe in it."

This statement I signed.

The temptation of Satan had been resisted, and I patted myself inwardly on the back and rejoiced at having a clear head once more. I had good need of it too, for Miss Helena's next question was what did I actually mean by a "Socialist conception of the future of humanity"?

This question called for an academic dissertation, and I was about to launch forth on one. But the three Phalangists were hardly a sympathetic audience for my passionate rhetorical efforts. The young lady cut me short and suggested the lapidary formula:

"Believes in Socialism to give workers chance."

She said Americans understood things the better the more briefly they were put.

In God's name, I said, Amen.

Then she asked me how I could account for the fact that I had stayed in Malaga after the Reds had gone.

I tried to explain with, as far as possible, American brevity, the whole complicated story of Sir Peter, Alfredo's car, and the whole apocalyptic atmosphere in Malaga. I myself felt that it did not sound very convincing.

But she was courteous enough not to express any doubts, and I asked her what had happened to Sir Peter.

She told me that he too was in prison. This was untrue; Sir Peter had by this time long since been on English soil and was moving heaven and earth to secure my release. But that was precisely what I was not to be told.

On leaving, my fellow journalist of the Hearst Press further told me that she worked with Captain Bolín in the Press and Propaganda Department at the Salamanca headquarters, that Madrid was on the point of falling, and that she would try to arrange for me to be moved to a better prison. I said that I should be most grateful to her if she could do this, for General Queipo and I had a long-standing aversion to each other.

"Thank you so-o-o much," she said. The officers saluted once again with extreme politeness, and off went the three of them; and I sank exhausted on to my bed, which now smelt most unwontedly of some Parisian perfume.

I was incapable of collecting my thoughts. Death sentence, life-long imprisonment, the correspondent of the Hearst Press, the Propaganda Department, the Phalangist uniform and the perfume were altogether too much for my poor head.

XIII

THE visit of the correspondent of the Hearst Press acting on behalf of the Propaganda Department—or should I say the visit of the female Phalangist acting on behalf of the Hearst Press—to whose competence I pay full tribute—took place on February 19th. It was the only official contact I had, during the course of three months, with the authorities who held me prisoner.

The day after this visit I felt enormous relief. The second day I remembered the fateful "might possibly"; the third day it became an obsession.

Doubt is a bacillus that eats slowly but surely into the brain; the patient positively feels the dirty little beast grazing on his grey matter. But in every long-drawn-out illness the patient eventually reaches a stage in which he has, although not reconciled himself to the pain, at least succeeded in arriving at a *modus vivendi* with it; he knows how to behave when the attack comes on. Mental misery likewise comes on in spasms; it is only in bad novels that people are in a permanent state of unhappiness for the whole twenty-four hours of the day. The daily routine of life, even of life in a condemned cell, cannot sustain for long the melodrama of despair; it banishes the agony to the dungeons of the consciousness. From there it makes itself heard only as a muffled bass in the symphony of the daily round and produces a vague feeling of uneasiness. Uneasiness and not unhappiness is the most common form of human suffering. Until an acute attack comes on.

Then the lock-gates give way and the boiling torrent of despair invades the consciousness. You will have to kneel down before the wall, they will shoot darkness into thine eyes.

Into the midst of thy thoughts, into the soft, warm cradle of thought they will send the annihilating lead.

When the drill touches the nerve of fear, the patient loses control of himself. The onslaught has begun. It is unbearable, one cannot stand it for long. One has to take a pill.

Every man needs a different pill to help him to arrive at a *modus vivendi* with his misery. Job cursed God when his sores festered; the prisoners in Malaga sang the "International." I, too, had my pills, a whole collection of various sorts of them, from the equation of a hyperbola and "my fill of days" to every kind of synthetic product of the spiritual pharmacy.

One of my magic remedies was a certain quotation from a certain work of Thomas Mann's; its efficacy never failed. Sometimes, during an attack of fear, I repeated the same verse thirty or forty times, for almost an hour, until a mild state of trance came on and the attack passed. I knew it was the method of the prayer-mill, of the African tom-tom, of the age-old magic of sounds. Yet in spite of my knowing it, it worked.

A similar effect to that of these anæsthetizing exercises I could obtain by the opposite method, that is, by sharp abstract speculation. I would start a train of thought deliberately at some given point, such as Freud's theories about death and the nostalgia for death; after a few minutes a state of feverish exaltation was evoked, a kind of running amok in the realm of reasoning, which usually ended in a day-dream. After a while I became sober again and the attack had passed.

The healing power of both methods was derived from the same device: that of merging that stark image of the firing-squad with the general problem of life and death, of merging my individual misery with the biological misery of the universe; just as the vibrations and tensions of a wireless-receiver are conducted to earth, where they disperse; I had "earthed" my distress.

In other words I had found out that the human spirit is able to call upon certain aids of which, in normal circumstances, it has no knowledge, and the existence of which it only discovers in itself in abnormal circumstances. They act, according to the particular case, either as merciful narcotics or ecstatic stimulants. The technique which I developed under the pressure of the death-sentence consisted in the skilful exploitation of these aids. I knew, by the way, that at the decisive moment when I should have to face the wall, these mental devices would act automatically, without any conscious effort on my part. Thus I had actually no fear of the moment of execution; I only feared the fear which would precede that moment. But I relied on the feeling I had experienced on the staircase in Sir Peter's house, while waiting for Bolín's shot; that dream-like feeling of having one's consciousness split in two, so that with one half of it one observes oneself with comparative coolness and aloofness, as though observing a stranger. The consciousness sees to it that its complete annihilation is never experienced. It does not divulge the secret of its existence and its decay. No one is allowed to look into the darkness with his eyes open; he is blindfolded beforehand.

This is why situations lived through are never so bad in reality as in imagination. Nature sees to it that trees do not grow beyond a certain height, not even the trees of suffering.

The days went by.

Friday, Saturday, Sunday, Monday, Tuesday, Wednesday, Thursday, Friday.

It was on Friday that I had received the visitors who brought the momentous news; from then to the next Friday the entries in my prison calendar are blank—no memorable event took place.

By memorable events are understood, in the murky bell-jar of prison, things like getting potato soup instead of bean soup for the midday meal, a few privately exchanged words with the warder or the orderly, a cigarette given one by the warder, a spider in the window, or a bug in the bed. These are breath-taking experiences, they employ and stimulate the free-running mechanism of thought for hours at a time. They are substitutes for visits to the movies, making love, reading the newspapers and the cares of daily life. Storms in teacups are, for those whose horizon extends no farther than the rim of the cup, quite as real as storms at sea.

The seven blank spaces on my calendar represented, then, the most absolute degree of uneventfulness imaginable. Nothing, not the least thing, not the least fraction of the least thing, happened which might cause the faintest breath of air to stir the idle sails of the windmill of time. Just as the bear, hibernating, feeds on his own fat, so did I, in my head, feed from the dishes of thirty years of reading, learning and living. But my brain was drained dry and the few drops of thought that I squeezed out of it were pale, like thrice-brewed tea.

It is a peculiar mechanism, the brain; it manufactures only if a market through the medium of the word or the pen is assured it beforehand. If there is no demand for its products, it goes on strike. One can fool it for a time by pretending to oneself to be the public; but it soon sees through the swindle. One's own ego is by no means an entertaining companion. After six weeks of solitary confinement I was so sick of myself that I only spoke to myself in formal terms and addressed myself as "Sir."

The astonishing thing, the puzzling thing, the consoling thing about this time was that it passed. I am speaking the plain unvarnished truth when I say that I did not know how. I tried to catch it in the act. I lay in wait for it, I riveted my eyes on the second hand of my watch, resolved to think of nothing else but pure time. I held it like the simpleton in the fable who thought that to catch a bird you had to put salt on its tail. I stared at the second hand for minutes on end, for quarters of an hour on end, until my eyes watered with the effort of concentration and a kind of trance-like stupor set in —and what I did not know afterwards was how long a time I had been observing its passing.

Time crawled through this desert of uneventfulness as though lame in both feet. I have said that the astonishing and consoling thing was that in this pitiable state it should pass at all. But there was something that was more astonishing, that positively bordered on the miraculous, and that was that this time, these interminable hours, days and weeks, passed *more swiftly* than a period of times has ever passed for me before. . . .

I was conscious of this paradox whenever I scratched a fresh mark on the white plaster of the wall, and with a particular shock of astonishment when I drew a circle round the marks to celebrate the passage of the weeks and, later, the months. What, another week, a whole month, a whole quarter of a year! Didn't it seem only like yesterday that this cell door had banged to behind me for the first time?

I racked my brain in an effort to explain to myself these paradoxes of time, while I paced up and down between my bunk and the W.C.—six and a half paces there, six and a half paces back. Gradually it dawned on me that those days which, owing to their uneventfulness and dreariness, seem longest, shrink to nothing as soon as they have become the past, precisely because of their uneventfulness. In the perspective of the past they have no extension, no volume, no specific gravity; they become geometric points, a diminishing vacuum, nothing. The greater the sum of blank days, the lighter their weight in the memory. The time that, when it is the present, passes most slowly, passes swiftest of all in the memory.

And the converse is also true. When events pile one upon the other and time gallops—then and only then is the span of time traversed cherished in all its details in the memory. The periods that pass most swiftly are in the memory the slowest.

It is in flight that time leaves behind the most visible traces. It is truly a strange will-o'-the-wisp, this time. If we experience time of such a quality that we have to look with a yawn at our watch, to count the minutes, as soon as its existence is brought to our consciousness—we may be sure that it will be extinguished in the memory. The only time that is unforgettable is that time during which one forgets that time exists. Only that time is fertile which remains chaste and unsullied by the touch of consciousness. . . .

Speculating on the subject of time was one of my favourite nostrums, and at times the only remedy that could help me to while it away. There was a bizarre consolation in the knowledge that these interminable, torturing hours, as soon as they had ceased to be the present, would shrink to nothing, like an india-rubber pig when the air escapes from it with a squeak. It was a constant swimming against the stream; the agony lifted as it converted itself into the past; one remained always at the same spot in the river, but all that was floating downstream was vanquished and overcome.

This time problem is the main problem of existence for every prisoner. And not only the prisoner, but of everyone who exists in unnatural, confined, conditions; in sanatoria, in the colonies. Often, very often, I found myself thinking of the "everlasting soup" in Thomas Mann's *Magic Mountain,* and the marvellous reflections on Time indulged in by his young hero in the hermetically sealed and isolated world of a sanatorium for consumptives; he, too, a captive, held prisoner not by social, but by biological, chaos.

. . . Saturday, Sunday, Monday, Tuesday, Wednesday, Thursday, Friday.

". . . The wind goeth towards the south, and turneth about unto the north; it whirleth about continually, and the wind returneth again according to his circuits. All the rivers run into the sea; yet the sea is not full. . . ."

While I was living down the eight blank days on my calendar and speculating upon time, out in the courtyard outside my window, the courtyard of the leap-froggers and football-players, thirty-seven men were shot.

But I did not know this at the time.

XIV

THERE were one or two individuals whom, when they entered the courtyard in the morning, my eyes greeted as old acquaintances. One was the old grandpapa who, rain or shine, always wore his fine woolly coat and paced up and down in the shadow of the wall with a book in his hand which he never read. Another was a twelve- or thirteen-year-old boy, dirty and delightful; his companions called him *cariño*, darling. Then there was Pedro, a semi-imbecile who played the part of the village idiot; the others would cuff him, trip him up and even spit at him—drawing-room manners were at a discount in the patio. Pedro seemed to enjoy this treatment; he would fall clownishly on all fours, and, highly flattered, wipe the spittle from his face—until quite unexpectedly he would fly into a temper, chase his tormentors, shake his fist at them and let forth a volley of abuse. The first time I saw this little scene it revolted me; then I too, like the others, came to welcome it as a diversion.

In the very first few days after my arrival in Seville I had been particularly struck by one of the prisoners—a thick-set man with a squint who wore a foreign-looking pullover with the red-yellow-red stripe of an official sewn on to it. He walked about with a certain air of condescension amongst the peasants in their faded linen smocks, and associated for the most part with the "dandies." I tried to guess his profession, and decided that he must be a professional boxer. He was the librarian.

I realized this a few days later when I saw him handing out books to the others in the patio.

All my efforts to get something to read had hitherto failed.

Nevertheless, with dogged persistence, three times a day, at mealtimes, I pegged away at my list of requests, which was now headed by the request for a book. The warders responded in various ways; one with indifference, another with a hypocritical *"mañana,"* or *"ahora,"* a third by slamming the door; the net result was always the same.

Then I began to make signs to the fat boxer outside. On the average he came past my window three times every morning and three times every afternoon during his perambulations; I lay in wait for hours for this moment in the hope of attracting his attention. At last, after nine or ten days, I succeeded; he looked across at me and nodded his head almost imperceptibly to signify that he had grasped what I wanted.

I waited in a state of excitement the whole afternoon for his appearance in my cell. I speculated greedily as to what would be the first book he would bring me. I waited until the evening and then all the next day, continuing to make signs which he either did not see or refused to see; and then waited another whole day. At last, on Saturday, February 27th, when I had given up all hope, my lucky moment arrived. During the midday meal the fat librarian came down the corridor past the open door of my cell.

I called out to him, and in my agitation spilt my soup at Angelkin's feet.

The librarian stood irresolutely in the corridor, but I was in luck, for one of the nice warders happened to be on duty and he signified that he had no objection to my borrowing a book. The librarian had a whole pile under his arm, and he gave me the top one. It was a Spanish translation of John Stuart Mill's autobiography.

And squeezed under the cover was a half-squashed cigarette.

It was a red-letter day—a real red-letter day. A day that must be celebrated with due ceremony.

I went on eating my beans deliberately, washed my bowl

with special care, and put it in the window alcove to dry. Then I sat down on the bed, lit the cigarette and began to read.

I read devoutly and fervently—and very slowly. I could not make out at least a quarter of the words, and, having no dictionary, I had to ponder the meaning of each sentence. But this only increased my enjoyment. I learned to read anew, with a long since forgotten concentration on every sentence, every adjective; I felt like someone who has been bed-ridden and who in learning to walk anew is acutely conscious of the play of his muscles. I fancy the Romans must have read in this fashion when books were written by hand on long parchment rolls; devoutly, sentence by sentence, only a few inches of the roll a day, so as to keep the rest for the morrow. When writers were obliged to use parchment rolls they knew how carefully people read them, and had confidence in their readers. Nowadays readers may have confidence in the writer, but writers have no confidence in the reader.

It was, incidentally, a particularly happy chance that it was John Stuart Mill's autobiography which lay on the top of the librarian's pile. I have always believed that in the administration of Divine Providence there is a special department entirely concerned with seeing that the right book comes into the hands of a reader at the right moment.

A Hemingway or a Joyce or a Huxley would have had a positively devastating effect at that particular moment. But here I stood at the foot of one of those monumental pillars of the monumental nineteenth century, a man whose life was an outstanding example of that kind of creative puritanism, free from crabbed self-complacency, which regards abstemiousness not as an end in itself but as necessary for the attainment of a spiritual object. He was, indeed, a pillar of strength, this old nineteenth-century figure; you could walk round him and tap the weatherproof stone with the palm of your hand, your face turned upwards to where he vanished in austere architectural perspectives—a position of the head that is exceedingly becoming to the mind.

The second book that I was given to read was De Maistre's *Voyage autour de ma Quartier*, and the first sentence that leaped to my gaze as I turned the pages was the soliloquy of the author, imprisoned in his room, as he surveys his library:

"They have forbidden me to go to and from the town and to move about freely in space; but they have left the entire universe at my disposal; its boundless, infinite space and infinite time are at my service. . . ."

The prison library contained about sixteen hundred for the most part very good books. They had been got together in the Republican era, and the new inquisitors had up till now forgotten to carry out a purge. There were even revolutionary pamphlets dating from the years 1930–1931, biographies of Caballero, Azaña and so forth.

This was typical of the whole prison. Everything was still carried on at the old jog-trot—a very Republican, very humane and very Spanish, slovenly jog-trot. Ninety-five per cent of the warders and subordinate officials belonged to the old personnel. They were steeped in the humane routine of the Republic, and their sympathy with the new régime was unlikely to be very great, even though some of them had, willy-nilly, to assume Phalangist uniforms. With three exceptions, all the warders were kindly and humane, some of them even unusually nice—in so far as their instructions would allow. And sometimes they would even disregard their instructions.

Somehow this vast prison made one think of the realm of the Sleeping Beauty in the midst of the turmoil of war. I heard later that it sometimes happened that, twenty-four hours before his execution, a prisoner would be sent up for a medical examination, and be ordered a milk-diet because of suspected appendicitis. The inertia of routine showed itself to be more powerful than the forces of the present; tradition contemptuously outlived death. It was an extremely humane, positively comfortable prison—picnics were held by the open gravesides.

All this was true of the warders and subordinates, who were in close and constant contact with the prisoners without having any say as to their fate. The higher you went in the hierarchy the more bleak, the more cold the atmosphere. To Spanish Generals no man below the rank of sergeant is a human being. For us inhumanity began with the sergeant.

In prison the sergeant is represented by the *"jefe de servicio,"* the head warder. For my first acquaintanceship with a head warder I had to thank, symbolically enough, a defect in the flushing of the W.C.

This was on the 28th, the day after I had been given my first book.

In the morning the cistern began to leak. I was too absorbed in John Stuart Mill to bother much about it. By the time the midday soup arrived the whole cell was wet. I drew the warder's attention to this and he promised—*ahora, ahora*—to send the *fontanero*, the plumber, along. In the meantime I was to mop the flags with the floor-cloth.

I did this, and then went back to John Stuart Mill. The plumber did not come, of course. By dusk the water was several millimetres deep on the cell-floor and the cistern was leaking worse than ever. By the time the evening soup arrived I no longer had any need to draw the warder's attention to the state of affairs; he could see the extent of the damage for himself. *"Ahora,"* he said kindly, "I'll send the *fontanero* along." But in the meantime I was to mop the cell with the floor-cloth so that the water did not overflow into the corridor.

I did this, cursing, but by now a steady rivulet of water was pouring from the cistern and by the second bugle-call the water was almost ankle-deep. Since the plumber had still not come, I began to drum furiously on the door—a proceeding which is forbidden after the last post has sounded.

After some time of persistent drumming the door flew open and in stormed the *jefe de servicio*, followed by a trembling Angelito.

The *jefe* was short and fat; he filled his Phalangist uniform to bursting-point and yet it was crinkled, like the skin of a badly filled sausage. He had a scar on his face that began at the nose and reached to the right ear, half of which was missing. He was not a prepossessing sight. He roared until the walls shook.

"What have you been up to here?" he thundered.

I said that the cistern was to blame, not I.

"You're only to speak when you are spoken to," he roared. "And when I come in, you've got to stand to attention over there by the wall."

I waded over to the wall and stood to attention. The *jefe* flung his cigarette-end irately on to the floor. The stump was peacefully swirled out of the door by the current.

"Mop the floor," bellowed the *jefe*.

I said that I had mopped the floor three times already (it was only twice), but that it had been of no use.

The *jefe* said that if he ordered it I had got to mop the floor six, ten, or twenty times, to mop it all day and all night; he brandished his rubber truncheon under my nose and promised to order me a *"flagelación"* the next day. Then, spitting into the flood, he strode out, banging the door behind him.

I set about drying the floor once more. Before I had finished the door opened and in came Don Ramón, one of the nicest of the warders, followed by the plumber. He put his finger to his lips and grinned. I realized that he had smuggled in the plumber after the "last post" against the *jefe's* orders and the prison regulations.

This incident had given me my first introduction to the ruling class of the prison. Thanks to the happy ending, however, it had taught me a useful lesson. I reflected that the *fontanero* would never have come if I had not kicked up a row; consequently, I thought to myself, I shall get my list of requests—from Consul to cigarettes—attended to soonest if I make a fuss. I waited one more day, reciting my list with particular importunity at each mealtime—and then, finding that I was again fobbed off with *"mañana"* and *"ahora,"* on Tuesday, the 2nd March, I began my first hunger strike.

The effect was beyond all expectation immediate.

When, in the morning, Don Ramón appeared with Angelito and the vat of coffee, I announced that I did not want anything. Don Ramón asked me if I had a stomach-ache. I said that I wished to speak to the Governor, and that I refused to touch any food until he arrived.

Don Ramón seemed very surprised, and Angelito grinned. They went away without a word.

At midday I again refused food. A different warder was on duty; he said nothing, but simply banged the door and went away. The matter must therefore already have got round. This seemed a favourable omen.

At six o'clock in the evening the door flew open and a solemn procession entered my cell. At the head the Governor, then the head warder, then Angelito, and finally one of the "dandies."

The Governor was a meagre, not unkindly little man. I learned later that he belonged to the old staff. They had not dared to sack him, for his knowledge of the workings of the prison had made him indispensable, but they had stuck a Phalangist officer right under his nose and had limited his sphere of action to purely technical matters.

The Governor looked at me for a while and then asked what was the matter with me, at the same time signing to the "dandy" to act as interpreter. I said that I knew enough Spanish to make myself understood, but he replied that he preferred to have an interpreter, so that he might get everything quite clear.

The little man inspired confidence. I briefly told him my case and came out with my list of requests. He said that he had to abide by his orders; I was *"incomunicado"* and might therefore neither write letters nor get in touch with the Consul. He had no say, either, he said, as to my future fate. But he would try to get my confiscated money returned to me and would try to see that I got those purely technical alleviations that lay within his power. In return I was to undertake to eat again.

I did this, and the procession marched out. But I buttonholed the "dandy" in the doorway, and managed to cadge a one-peseta voucher from him to buy cigarettes.

I waited impatiently to see whether the Governor would keep his word, or whether he too was one of the *"mañana"* type.

But the very next morning in came Angelito, accompanied by Don Ramón, with an armful of the most fabulous treasures. He laid them all out on the bed, and the two of them stood by with benevolent expressions on their faces as though about to distribute presents from a Christmas tree. I was positively dazzled, and I examined each object minutely and lovingly. There were in all:

> a stump of pencil,
> five sheets of white paper,
> a piece of soap,
> a face-towel,
> a shirt.

Don Ramón explained that the paper and pencil were not for writing letters, but for "composing," for the Governor thought that if I were allowed to "compose" again it would "lighten my heart." Then he added, with a wink, that since everything that I wrote might be taken away at any time to be examined, I had better write only "nice things."

I promised to write only nice things. Once more I had that exalted feeling of overwhelming, boundless joy that I had had when the barber had come, and when I had been given my first book.

I debated with myself which luxury I should sample first, the pencil or the soap. The soap won; I scrubbed myself from top to toe, put on the new shirt, washed out the old one and laid it in the window alcove to dry.

Then it was the turn of the pencil.

My diary dates from this day onwards. Bearing in mind the fact that I was "to write only nice things" I worded it in the style of the "Uncle-Bertie-seriously-ill-inform-Auntie" tele-gram. If at night ten prisoners were shot, I wrote: "Woke at ten, bad dreams."

My diary of the last days of Malaga, which was confiscated on my arrest, I reconstructed from memory, as also the events of the first three weeks after my arrest.*

By a particularly happy accident I managed to smuggle this diary out of prison when I was released. The following entries are for the most part unchanged; I have simply translated the flowery language back to normal speech and in places amplified the entries.

* Out of a sense of pedantry I should mention here that one or two dates in the series of articles which I published after my release in the *News Chronicle* are not quite correct. The luggage containing my diary was not at hand at the moment, and I therefore got the dates of certain events mixed up. The accounts of the events themselves were in no way affected by this.

XV

Wednesday, March 3rd.

Morning received pencil, paper, soap, towel, shirt. If I only had a toothbrush I should almost be a human being again.

At breakfast gave Angelito the dandy's voucher for one peseta to get me eight packets "Hebras" cigarettes and four boxes matches from canteen. He said prison canteen not open till eleven. Spent morning copying out extracts from Mill. Write almost microscopically to save paper.

Midday still no cigarettes. Angelito off duty, vanished, and with him the peseta.

Read all afternoon. When evening soup came got cigarettes. Angel says no more cheap "Hebras" in canteen; bought one packet "Especiales," twenty for 80 cmos., one box of matches for 5 cmos. Didn't want to return vouchers for remaining 15 cmos., said a little *propina* (tip) was due to him on every purchase. Told him no tip till I got back my confiscated money. Answered: "You can wait till you're blue in the face," but finally forked out the 15 cmos.

Thursday, March 4th.

Morning finished John Stuart Mill. Tried to signal to librarian through window that wanted book changed, but no use.

Am rationing cigarettes. Yesterday smoked four, night two, twelve left—want to make them last three days. Perhaps by then my money will come.

Evening.

Signalled librarian all afternoon. No use. At seven taken to prison office. Secretary showed me telegram from Salamanca to Governor:

"Governor provincial prison Seville stop money personal effects prisoner Koestler with Colonel Fuster General Staff Second Division Seville stop Bolín"

So Bolín returned to Salamanca? This is reassuring.

Secretary informs me Governor has written to Colonel Fuster requesting him to send my money and luggage to prison.

Long live the Governor.

On way back from office passed Cell 44. Card with Caballero's name still there, but 42 and 43 no longer have cards. Wonder what has happened to inmates.

Whole day signalled librarian. No use. Money and luggage not yet arrived. Midday fish soup with boiled lettuce leaves. Seven cigarettes left.

Saturday, March 6th.

Morning tried to signal librarian. No use. Got into a rage and chain-smoked all seven cigarettes. Money and luggage not arrived.

Midday handed over to Angelito last 15 cmo. voucher. At five he bought one cigar at 10 cmos. and one box matches. Smoked three puffs, then put it out. Five puffs after supper. Still have almost half left. To-morrow is Sunday, so money *can't* come.

Sunday, March 7th.

Morning Mass in the gallery outside my cell. Watched through spy-hole prisoners marching along four abreast. During Mass three or four faces remained in my field of vision.

All peasants; seemed to have little interest in the service. Then sermon; i e., front-line news rather than sermon. Could only understand about half. Parson threatened all "Reds" with eternal damnation. Said still time to recant. Observed effect on those in my field of vision. Listeners exchanged cigarettes, picked their noses, spat discreetly on floor.

On march back priest passed for a second time through my field of vision. Short, swarthy, greasy fellow, type of army padre in Great War.

Afternoon librarian arrived unexpectedly, brought De Maistre's *Voyage autour de ma Quartier*. In my delight smoked. rest of cigar, kept stump to chew tobacco. Chewing quite good substitute.

Monday, March 8th.

Such craving to smoke that I ate up entire cigar-stump.

Three fantastic new arrivals in patio. They are respectably dressed—lawyers, I imagine, or doctors or something—but all three have long black beards and are deathly pale, literally as white as a sheet. Embraced several other prisoners on entering courtyard; all three wept. Imagine must have been long time in solitary confinement and were being let out in patio for first time. I suppose I must look just as fantastic—to-morrow whole month of isolation up.

Asked warder midday if I might write to Governor requesting him to press for my money and luggage. Warder said Governor was taken to hospital yesterday for serious operation. Advised me not to write to his substitute.

Given up all hope of getting back things. Is better, too. Hoping means waiting, and waiting makes one nervy.

Wednesday, March 10th.

Yesterday first month of imprisonment over.

Am incapable of visualizing future at all concretely, despite constant speculation and forging plans. But all plans are somehow dreamlike, unreal. All thought more and more takes form of day-dreaming. Whenever cell door opens fresh air from the corridor makes me dizzy and I have to hold on to the table.

If a warder addresses a word to me I grow hoarse with excitement.

Finished De Maistre overnight; ever since early morning signalled vainly again at window. Librarian seems purposely to avoid looking over here, perhaps because too lazy to bring a book. Surely he must have enough imagination to realize what a book means to a man in solitary confinement. I had imagined more solidarity among political prisoners.

Out in the patio they are starting to build a lavatory. They are building with bricks, right in the middle.

Have awful cravings for tobacco. Believe everything would be bearable if I had a cigarette. Tried to cadge one from Angel at supper-time. Says he has none, while all the time his pocket is full of them. But he calls me "Arturito" and at every opportunity pats me affectionately on the back.

Thursday, March 11th.

When the prisoners are led out into the patio and when they come back, they march four abreast along the corridor past my cell. They walk slowly, with shuffling steps; most of them wear felt slippers or bast sandals; I stand at my spy-hole and follow the procession with my eyes, as one face after another comes within my field of vision. All have a habit of reading out the name-cards on the cell doors as they pass. Often I hear my name spelled out in undertones fifteen or twenty times in succession: "Ar-tu-ro-ko-est-ler." Sometimes one of them will read the rest, too: "*In-co-mu-ni-ca-do. O-jo.*" "*O-jo*" means: "keep an eye on him." Sometimes, when I am absorbed in reading or lost in a reverie, the sudden murmuring of my name seems to come from a chorus of ghosts.

To-day midday, as they came in for siesta, someone threw a piece of paper into my cell as if in fun. . . .

(London, Autumn, 1937.)

It was a piece of brown paper screwed up into a ball. Unfolding it, I read the following lines:

"Comrade, we know that you are here and that you are a friend of the Spanish Republic. You have been condemned to death; but they will not shoot you. They are much too afraid of the new King of England. They will only kill us—the poor and humble (los pobres y humildes).

"Yesterday again they shot seventeen in the cemetery. In our cell, where there were once 100 there are now only 73. Dear comrade foreigner, we three are also condemned to death, and they will shoot us to-night or to-morrow. But you may survive; and if you ever come out you must tell the world all about those who kill us because we want liberty and no Hitler.

"The victorious troops of our Government have conquered Toledo and have also got Oviedo, Vitoria and Badajoz. And soon they will be here, and will carry us victoriously through the streets. Further letters will follow this one. Courage. We love you.

"THREE REPUBLICAN MILITIAMEN."

No further letters followed. I learned later that two of the men were shot that very night, and the third, whose sentence was commuted, was sentenced to thirty years' penal servitude—the Spanish equivalent to a life term.

I had to learn that letter by heart. It has literally become a part of my body, for half an hour after I received it my cell was visited by the guard of inspection. I had no time to tear up the note, and so was obliged to swallow it.

Friday, March 12th.

Morning librarian. Brought Agatha Christie's *Muerte en las Nubes* (Death in the Clouds). An old usuress is bumped off in an aeroplane with a poisoned Indian blowpipe. . . .

Out in the patio the poor and humble are still playing football and leap-frog. Impossible to discover if any are missing, and which.

My paper is coming to an end; am writing so small that my eyes water.

Saturday, March 13th.

Yesterday evening one of the imprisoned Moors sang again. The song consisted of two words, repeated over and over again: "Ya la-ee-lay—ya la-ee-lay"—Oh night! I have often heard it in Syria and Irak, the camel-drivers sing it as they trot behind their beasts at night. Always the same two words, plaintively drawn out.

Then I had a visit from a little black cat. She leaped up on to my window-sill from the courtyard. Should have loved to have her in my cell, but she couldn't get in because of the wire nettting, and I couldn't even stroke her. She went off in disappointment and sprang on to the next window-sill—No. 42. Apparently she found the night too cold and wanted to find a cosy hiding-place. She could get in nowhere and wailed half the night like a baby. She must have thought the people living in this house very unfriendly to stretch queer wire netting over their windows expressly to prevent little cats from climbing in.

To-day the little black cat was in patio the whole day long, and another, a white one. Everyone was kind to them—much kinder than to poor Pedro, our village idiot. He flew into one of his rages again.

Afternoon pouring rain, courtyard empty.

Evening. Still raining. Large puddles have formed in the courtyard, almost ponds.

To-day four weeks since my arrival here.

Sunday, March 14th.

Again unable to sleep. Got up about one and looked out into the courtyard. The rain had stopped, the stars were reflected in the black puddles. It was so still that I could hear frogs croaking—from somewhere outside probably. This gave me the illusion of being in open country.

Morning, Mass again, but this time no sermon. Perhaps news from front is unfavourable and divine inspiration absent. I wonder what's happening in the world outside. Sometimes I think perhaps the world war has already broken out. My socks are completely done for.

Midday new warder; a bull-dog with brutal, fleshy features. Bears a striking resemblance to Charles Laughton as Captain Bligh in *Mutiny on the Bounty*.

Signalled to librarian all day. No good.

This afternoon was suddenly transferred to next cell, No. 40. Was not told why. Fittings precisely the same, only the view of the courtyard slightly different. Feel strange and ill-at-ease in the new cell. Miss familiar scratches on the wall.

Monday, March 15th.

Morning librarian. Brought Stevenson's *The Adventures of David Balfour* and five fresh sheets of paper. Tried to borrow a peseta from him; but he said he had nothing himself. Gave me a cigarette—the first for days. Smoking first made me drunk, then sea-sick.

Midday they forgot to bring me food, perhaps because in new cell. Drummed on the door till fists ached; finally at four got a bowl of beans, not from the big vat, but straight in the bowl. Suspected that it had been scraped together from the leavings, but ate it all the same.

Now the bull-dog is on duty all the time. This is very depressing. Hitherto the warders have sometimes said a kind word when bringing meals, such as: "Eat up, Arturito, and get fat," or something of the kind, and the cheering effect of a few words like that would keep me going for an hour or two. The whole mood of a night or an afternoon depends on

the tone of voice of Angelito or the warder when they bring
me food. I react to friendly or unfriendly waves like a seismo-
graph.
The bull-dog has a terribly depressing effect.

Night.

Despite all my feelings of self-respect I cannot help looking
on the warders as superior beings. The consciousness of being
confined acts like a slow poison, transforming the entire character. This is more than a mere psychological change, it is not
an inferiority complex—it is, rather, an inevitable natural process. When I was writing my novel about the gladiators I always wondered why the Roman slaves, who were twice, three
times as numerous as the freemen, did not turn the tables on
their masters. Now it is beginning gradually to dawn on me
what the slave mentality really is. I could wish that everyone
who talks of mass psychology should experience a year of
prison.

I had never believed the saying that a dictatorship or a
single person or a minority can maintain its ascendancy by
the sword alone. But I had not known how living and real
were those atavistic forces that paralyse the majority from
within.

I did not know how quickly one comes to regard a privileged stratum of men as beings of a higher biological species
and to take their privileges for granted as though they were
natural endowments. Don Ramón has the key and I am in the
cage; Don Ramón, as well as I, looks upon this state of things
as entirely natural and is far from regarding it as in any way
an anomaly.

And if a crazy agitator were to come and preach to us that
all men are equal, we should both laugh him to scorn; Don
Ramón with all his heart, I, it is true, only half-heartedly—
but all the same I should laugh.

Tuesday, March 16th.

Another week gone. Five weeks since the day of my arrest. And almost four weeks since the state-visit of the Hearst girl. If Franco had commuted the death sentence surely they would have let me know.

But it's doubtful whether they would also let me know of refusal to commute. In that case does one not hear that one's sentence is confirmed until the last moment?

After all, I was never told of the Malaga court-martial sentence.

Vaguely I recall precedents. Hauptmann, for example, Lindbergh baby murderer, learned of the rejection of his appeal only twenty-four hours before going to the chair. Don't know which is preferable. Fancy preferable not to hear until the last moment.

The beastliest thing of all would be not to be informed of the commutation at all; to be left for months or years in uncertainty.

My mind has been following up this train of thought in all its permutations every day for the past week. Only wonder that my spirits are not much lower than they are. If ever I get out they'll all hold up their hands and say how dreadful it must have been. And all the time I shall have a knowing little feeling that, after all, everything was not *so* bad as they imagine. Funny how elastic the limits of what is bearable are.

During the first few days I actually counted my shirt-buttons: reprieved—shot—reprieved—shot. Then I gave it up because an unfavourable result always terrified me.

The joke is one can't ever completely convince oneself that the whole thing is reality and not an obscure game. Who really believes in his own death? I can't help thinking of Sir Peter's telling me that one should disinfect the hypodermic syringe before committing suicide, or else one would get an abscess. I fancy there must be some mathematic relationship;

one's disbelief in death grows in proportion to its approach.

I don't believe that since the world began a human being has ever died *consciously*. When Socrates, sitting in the midst of his pupils, reached out for the goblet of hemlock, he must have been at least half convinced that he was merely showing off. He must have seemed to himself to be rather bogus and have secretly wondered at his disciples' taking him so seriously. Of course he knew theoretically that the draining of the goblet would prove fatal; but he must have had a feeling that the whole thing was quite different from what his perfervid, humourless pupils imagined it; that there was some clever dodge behind it all known only to himself.

Of course everyone knows that he must die one day. But to know is one thing, to believe another.

If it were not so, how could I feel as I write this that the whole thing is a theoretical discussion which doesn't concern me in the least?

True, at least once a day there is a short-circuit in my consciousness, and for minutes on end I behold the reality in a full blaze of light, as though illumined by some psychical explosion.

Then no thoughts, no pills avail; only brute fear remains.

But it passes, everything passes; even the minute when one stands before the firing squad and the lead pierces its way through mouth and nose and eyes. And then it is all behind one.

So why get agitated, when it all passes?

Up to now I have kept myself under control and not written about these things. I must not do so again; it agitates me too much.

If only I could somehow get that little cat into the cell.

Wednesday, March 17th.

Have used up almost all the paper in two days. From now on will write things which have no connection with the diary (mathematics and other stuff) on the tiles above the wash-basin. Can be rubbed out later.

Great event in the afternoon; was taken to have a shower-bath. The prison-bathroom is positively luxurious. In addition to showers and baths there is a swimming pool. Of course almost nothing works now. The pool is empty and filthy, the bath-taps are out of order; only two cold showers function. But it was a marvellous feeling to be clean again. Lucky find in the pool: an old bit of toilet-soap.

Caballero still there; Cells 41 and 43 are empty, but on No. 42 there is a new Spanish name.

Thursday, March 18th.

The three newcomers in the patio have lost their black beards, and are shaven and already slightly sunburnt. Was glad to see a tall blond young fellow whom I have missed in the patio for some days reappear. Had feared. . . .

Finished Stevenson, enjoyed it tremendously. Marvellous how well English authors are translated into Spanish. Now the business of making signals to the *bibliotecario* starts all over again.

Friday, March 19th.

Early this morning asked again to be shaved; but they told me to-day is *fiesta*, holiday. Must be Good Friday. Easter will come and perhaps I shan't even notice it. . . .

There was a service again this morning and there was good fish soup at midday. We now have fish soup every Friday and sometimes there is a morsel of meat among the beans or potatoes.

At midday the librarian came and suddenly spoke French with a Parisian accent. I was very astonished since hitherto had not remarked foreign accent in his Spanish. Promised me new book for to-morrow, and advised me *"pas se faire de mauvais sang."* I would rather he lent me a peseta.

Later a new warder came into my cell; don't know what he

wanted; he laughed amiably and went off. A little later the new *jefe de servicio* came—Phalangist uniform, cold, formal. Asked him whether he could not do something about my money. Promised to let me know to-morrow.

Saturday, March 20th.

Angel brought me new book at the request of the librarian; Gabriel Miro's *The Cherries in the Cemetery.* Weak stuff, chit-chatty, sentimental. Through the window watched a couple of chaser 'planes leaping and looping in the blue air like young dolphins. Perfect symbol of freedom. Wondered what kind of world I should find if I came out of here in ten years' time without having had papers or news in the meantime. Made rapid survey of changes from nineteen twenty-seven to nineteen thirty-seven; much less difference than one might imagine.

Afternoon saw through spy-hole two black-clad women walking down the corridor, probably on some errand of mercy. One had finely chiselled Velasquez features; it was pleasant and comforting to see them; it is really strange how cut off one is here from half of humanity.

Late in the evening I heard some newcomers brought in; one cried; but I did not dare to look through the spy-hole.

Sunday, March 21st.

Rain, rain, the whole day. The courtyard is a swamp. Someone made a speech before Mass, but I could not understand it. Read and dreamed. I find myself sinking more and more into day-dreams—I lose myself for three or four hours on end, pacing up and down, up and down, in a half-dazed state.

Afternoon my watch stopped again. Got a terrible fright, but poked about in the works till it went again.

Monday, March 22nd.

In the night my bed collapsed—I found myself on the ground and dreamed that I had been shot. Confirms the curious phenomenon that the fraction of a second between crash and waking is enough to construct *post factum* an entire story. The sound of the crash is only admitted to consciousness by the time the story has been improvised—till then the crash must wait on the threshold of the consciousness.

This execution dream was an exception—as a rule I now have mainly pleasant dreams. Never before have they been so beautiful. Often I laugh when dreaming, and my laughter wakes me up. Beautiful animals, Grecian scenery, also beautiful girls, but asexual. Am apparently developing an old-maid mentality; when reading I rejoice if the heroine remains chaste and the rules of decency are observed (formerly, the contrary was true).

. . . Was reminded of my friend A. N., when he was being psycho-analysed. He seemed to me like a wounded horse dragging itself across the bull ring and trailing its entrails behind it. A far from pleasant sight.

Could not go to sleep again. Compared psycho-analysts to sewage-cleaners; the penetrating smell of their profession clings to them even in private life. In their eyes is always a look suggestive of spiritual sewage-cleaning.

Note with displeasure that I am becoming more and more malevolent in my solitude. Sentimental and malevolent.

Got three cigarettes from Angel at midday. Will try to smoke only one a day.

'Planes again. Heinkels and Capronis, with white crosses on tail fins. Seven of them.

Evening barber came; offmowed beard with haircutting machine. Asked him why not with razor; he said razor-shaving costs money.

Tuesday, March 23rd.

Actually have two cigarettes left, but no matches. Angel had none on him this morning. Promised me some midday. Only one sheet of paper left.

Wednesday, March 24th.

Smoked last cigarette at twelve. Once more have got obsession of button-counting. In walking up and down take care always to tread in middle of flagstones; if, after pacing up and down five times, haven't touched the line, I shall be reprieved. Often before had attacks of such compulsions, hitherto always managed to fight them down; to-day for first time let myself go.

Six weeks to-day since arrest.

Thursday, March 25th.

Got De Maistre's book for the second time; so read it for fourth time. Nice sentence: *"L'ange distributeur des pensées."*

At midday the warder surprised me with the fantastic announcement that my money would arrive in the afternoon. He advanced me two cigarettes. Waited in fever of impatience till evening, telling myself continually it was a mistake—from an involved superstitious belief that if I thought it a mistake, then it would be all right. At last the evening soup came. Asked warder; he laughed, said he had confused me with another English prisoner, who had now got his money. . . .

The other Englishman, it turns out, is the "dandy," who interpreted during the director's visit. He is a merchant from Gibraltar (Spaniard of British nationality), who is here for smuggling currency. Asked what he was doing with political prisoners. Warder said that in wartime currency manipulation is a political offence.

Friday, March 26th.

Grey day; nervy state, stomach-ache and melancholia.

At midday suddenly heard German spoken in the patio. Couldn't believe my ears. A thick-set, red-cheeked, blond young man in a blue mechanic's overall stood on the white taboo-line, obliquely opposite my window, speaking cautiously into Cell 37.

Then he paced up and down and kept calling out sentences in German to number 37 as he passed.

He wanted to write to his Consul, he said, but they wouldn't give him any paper.

He was in a cell with six others, he said, all lousy Spaniards.

They were all Reds here, he said; one had to be very careful.

I couldn't catch the replies from 37. Grasped only that the inmate of 37 must be called Carlos, spoke German and was an old friend of the blond fellow.

I wonder what it all means.

Have thrown my socks away; they were no longer wearable. My shirts and pants are only rags now; my suit, which also serves me as pyjamas, looks like a stage costume out of the Beggar's Opera.

Saturday, March 27th.

At midday offered to sell my watch to warder for hundred cigarettes. He refused. An hour later got first letter from D., and hundred pesetas.

I was really half-crazy with excitement. I embraced Angelito in presence of the warder and the prison secretary, who brought the letter.

Angelito grinned sourly all over his crinkled old woman's face, and was suddenly full of devotion and charm. He gave me ten cigarettes straight away as an advance against future tips; then they all marched off.

The letter is dated March the 8th—so it has taken twenty days to come.

It consists only of five or six cheering sentences, deliberately trivial in order to get past censor. It went in some mysterious way to the British Consul, Malaga, who passed it on to the Military Authorities, who forwarded it to the prison authorities. Whence it is obvious that my wife, despite all efforts, has so far been unable to discover my whereabouts. The last sentence says that I must without fail get a few words in my own handwriting to her via the consulate. From which I gather she certainly doesn't know whether I'm still alive or not.

Drummed on the door and asked whether I might answer the letter. The warder had obviously already received instructions on this point, for he said promptly I might not. I said I wanted to write only one sentence: that I was alive. He said it was impossible.

Then Angelito came to change the hundred peseta note into prison vouchers. He asked fawningly whether he could get me provisions from the canteen. With a lordly gesture I gave him fifteen pesetas, and told him to spend it for me, telling him he could deduct two pesetas for himself straight away.

A positively magical transformation has come about in our relations. Hitherto I have felt myself entirely in Angelito's power and dependent on his moods; now he is a poor devil and I a Señor. Must confess this cheap satisfaction gives me great pleasure.

With the evening soup he brought me a whole basketful of the most fabulous treasures. Cigarettes, matches, toothbrush, toothpaste, sardines in oil, sardines in tomato sauce, lettuce, vinegar, oil and salt in a special container, red paprika sausage, dried figs, cheese, Andalusian cakes, chocolate, tunnyfish in oil and four hard-boiled eggs. My bed was transformed into a delicatessen store. I poured my ration of lentils down the W.C. at one swoop, and devoured these luxuries in any order I fancied—chocolate and sardines, sausage and sweetmeats.

For the first time for six weeks I feel satisfied—satisfied, contented and tired.

If only I could get a word to D.

Sunday, March 28th.

Through Angelito bought socks, writing paper, basket to store my provisions and further delicacies. Day passed chiefly in eating and smoking. Librarian brought three little volumes of humorous sketches by Averchenko. In the afternoon the blond young German spoke to No. 37 again. Said he had got paper to write to his Consul and promised the invisible Carlos to lend him a peseta.

In the evening the bugler blew a new tune for the last post. An even more melancholy tune.

Monday, March 29th.

All my pleasure in eating and drinking has gone to the devil. Every bite reminds me of the origin of the money and the letter. These attacks of homesickness recur at short intervals and with a violence I've never before experienced. What a sad sort of creature one is; so long as one's hungry, one has no other desire but to eat and eat, but the moment one is replete the "nobler feelings" suddenly make themselves felt and spoil all one's pleasure. Three days ago a piece of cheese seemed to me the highest of all earthly gifts. Now, the moment I set eyes on a piece of cheese or a sardine tin, the thought of home inevitably occurs to me, and then there's the devil to pay. The good God has definitely put a few wheels too many in our heads.

Afternoon Angelito paid me a private visit and relieved me very willingly of a part of the cause of my misery by devouring sardines, cheese and chocolate. Afterwards the new *jefe de servicio* came to inform me that Colonel Fuster had not yet answered his inquiry about my confiscated money and luggage. Doesn't interest me now. Asked him when a decision as to my case was to be expected. Said he didn't know; I was an important case, one didn't capture a Red journalist every day. I was highly flattered, but wonder whether it's good or bad to be an important case.

Tuesday, March 30th.

I fancy the *jefe* only visited me because he had heard I'd got some money. It is really curious to see how my prestige has risen overnight and how my own self-confidence has grown since I've had some money.

Have sixty pesetas left; must begin to be careful.

Dreamed—for second time during imprisonment—that I was free. All rather colourless and disappointing.

Got Mill once more and made extracts whole day.

Wednesday, March 31st.

At midday the warder asked me whether I would like some wine. You bet I would. Got a big beaker full for 45 centimos —about half a pint. Learned that every prisoner has the right to buy wine for the midday and evening meals, but no more than this quantity . . . I keep the midday ration for evening, so as to drink both together. Tolerably good white wine, but too little to have any effect. All the same very good to have wine at all.

Thursday, April 1st.

Got Nerval's *Aurelia*, Bunin's *Puyodol* and Stevenson's *Olala* at same time. Now I have pretty good food, wine, cigarettes, clean underclothes and good books, no material worries, no bother with publishers, editors and colleagues. Soberly viewed, things are going quite well with me if it were not for my fear. I fancy that if my state of uncertainty came to an end, and later on I were to receive permission to be with the others in the patio, I should rub along quite well here.

When I read I forget everything for hours on end and am quite contented and really cheerful. Then I remember the letter and all the commiseration expressed in it and I have a feeling that I have a conventional obligation to be unhappy. I picture to myself how my wife must be picturing my situation and my commiseration reflects her commiseration like the echo of an echo. Again and again I catch myself being conscience-stricken at being so cheerful. Custom demands that a man in prison must suffer.

It must be very irksome for the dead to have the living think of them.

Friday, April 2nd.

What pearls one discovers in comparatively unknown books, when, as a result of unwonted circumstances, one forms the unwonted custom of reading attentively!

Gerard de Nerval spent half his life in a madhouse; he wrote the book that I am reading partly between two attacks of madness and partly during an attack; it contains page after page of completely absurd visions and the plot of the story is his own fluctuation between insanity and reason. At one point his condition seems definitely to improve, and his mind grows clear. The result is that he is now kicked out of the asylum and has to wander homeless through the streets of Paris in the cold winter nights, without a penny in his pockets and without an overcoat, instead of pursuing his gay visions in the well-heated madhouse. Half-dead with exhaustion he muses:

"When you regain what people call reason, its loss seems scarcely worth bemoaning."

At thirty-five he was found hanged.

I should like to know whether he hanged himself because, at the moment when he knotted the rope, he happened to be mad or because he happened to be sane.

The outside world becomes more and more unreal to me.

Sometimes I even think that I was happy before. One weaves illusions not only about one's future, but also about one's past.

Saturday, April 3rd.

Got needle and thread, spent the whole day cobbling the tattered remains of my shirt, my pants and my new socks. At midday got fresh lettuce from Angelito wrapped up in a scrap of old newspaper. Saw from it that King of the Belgians had been in Berlin and that Italy had concluded a pact with Jugoslavia; but nothing about the Spanish war. Was astonished and horrified to find how little this news affected me and how much my interest in what is happening outside is waning. And the second month is not yet up.

What interests me much more is that the siesta promenaders —Byron and the consumptive—have now got a companion. Lanky, unshaven, dirty, and wears glasses. Has on a short leather coat which looks much too small for him. His whole appearance is somehow comic and pathetic in its awkwardness; have no idea what he can be.

Sunday, April 4th.

Very bad day. Only a few hours' relief in sleeping and writing. My heart is giving me so much trouble that at times I feel as though I am suffocating. Whole day in bed in a kind of apathetic coma. The idea of getting up alarms me.

Have never been so wretched since Malaga.

Monday, April 5th.

Had heart attack during night, just like the one in 1932. Am very much afraid another one coming on.

XVI

THE bit about the heart attack was a fabrication.

It was a complicated plan for malingering, which I had thought out on the Sunday, when the barometer had once more reached its lowest point. The idea was to compel the authorities to transfer me to the prison hospital; in hospital, I thought, it must be a lot easier to find ways and means of getting in touch with the British Consul.

But I knew that it was difficult to deceive a prison doctor, and that I must therefore become really ill. To this end I resolved to go on hunger strike, not openly but secretly; to accept all food but surreptitiously to put it down the W.C. until I had become so weak that they would have to fetch a doctor. To the doctor I would then say that I suffered from heart trouble; this is the most difficult of all complaints in connection with which to spot malingering, and, besides, I knew that after ten to fifteen days of starvation the heart is weakened and the pulse becomes irregular.

Since I had constantly to be on the watch lest my diary should be examined, I took good care to see that its contents tallied with my plan of malingering. I therefore wrote, instead of "fasting" or "starvation"—heart attack. The diary thus acquired a sentimental tone that was bound to tear the heart-strings of the Spanish censor.

It was a childish scheme; but I had no other choice.

The following italicized passages have either been transcribed from my code or are later additions.

I began my fast on Monday, April 5th, eight weeks after my arrest.

Monday, April 5th (Evening).

Got Sterne's *Sentimental Journey* in Spanish.

"—If this won't turn out something,—another will;—no matter,
—'tis an assay upon human nature—I get my labour for my pains,
—'tis enough;—the pleasure of the experiment has kept my senses
and the best part of my blood awake, and laid the gross to sleep."

*But the gross part did not sleep, hunger kept it awake. I had
read somewhere that after three or four days of fasting the craving for food ceased. This prospect consoled me.*

Tuesday, April 6th.

Second day of heart trouble. In the afternoon the barber
came to my cell, and the warder sat down on the bed as usual
during the procedure and chattered. Discovered by means of
judicious questioning that Madrid has not yet fallen; warder
thinks the war will last a long time yet. Warder, barber and I
agreed that there should be no wars.

*Bread can't be put down the W.C. in one lump; I had to crum-
ble it up into little morsels and pull the plug two or three times
before it was all gone. In crumbling it I could smell whole corn-
fields, bursting with vitamins in the sun. Soup is easier, it goes
down at one swoop.*

Wednesday, April 7th.

Got Jules Verne's *Round the World in Eighty Days.*
Thought it would be fun, but it does not amuse me at all.
Either Verne is to blame or else my heart, which is constantly
giving me trouble. Am forced continually to think of it and
am incapable of concentrating on reading or writing for even
ten minutes at a time.

*I began to have day-dreams about food. I dreamed of beef-
steaks, potatoes and cheese with the same voluptuous fervour as
that with which schoolboys dream of film actresses. I fancy that
if the function of eating were so restricted and hedged about with*

taboos by society as the function of love, the psycho-analysts would have their work cut out to deal with repressed hunger-complexes and thirst neuroses. If a man dreamed of a violin it would signify that his dark instincts were yearning for a leg of mutton.

Thursday, April 8th.

Have made a discovery.

This afternoon the blond German had another conversation with the mysterious Carlos. He said that Carlos should write a letter to his Consul and put it on the window-ledge in the north corner of courtyard; he, the German, would then get it sent on for him. I wondered how on earth Carlos could do this when he was in an isolation cell.

Then during the siesta I saw the tall man with spectacles stroll casually to the window described and fumble about there. So the mysterious Carlos is identical with the new siesta-promenader.

Then, later in the afternoon, the German went and took the letter.

This has been my only distraction to-day. My heart is giving me such trouble that I am unable to read. The Devil take Phineas Fogg; his cold-bloodedness is a direct provocation.

I had thought that the craving for food ceased after four days. It doesn't.
Quite the contrary.

Friday, April 9th.

Two months to-day since Bolín appeared in Sir Peter's house with his revolver.

Have at last got rid of Phineas Fogg and have been given Tolstoy's *War and Peace.*

A new promenader has appeared in the patio during the siesta. A little Andalusian peasant with a wild black stubble of beard and soft, blue, slightly prominent eyes. He kept with

Byron and the consumptive; Carlos stalked around the court-yard by himself.

My heart no better; to-day the sixth day. . . .

Have thirty pesetas left. Shall buy no more extra provisions, only cigarettes and soap.

Ever since I have been ill time has passed appallingly slowly. Twice or three times as slowly as before. It not only limps, it drags a leaden weight behind it. This is because I am unable to read, to write, to concentrate—in brief, to forget time. This theorizing about time is gradually becoming an obsession. When I was still young in this prison I tried to lie in wait for the hands of my watch, to experience pure time. Now I know that an inexorable law prevails: increasing awareness of time slows down its pace, complete awareness of time would bring it to a standstill. Only in death does the present become reality; time freezes; he who succeeds in experiencing "pure time" experiences nothingness.

I had to take great care to see that my deception with regard to the food was not spotted. Not only did I throw away my rations, I also had to go on buying things from the canteen and to dispose of them bit by bit. My shortage of money at last gave me an excuse to rid myself of this additional torture.

Saturday, April 10th.

I have always thought it very funny when old ladies say that they cannot read war books, because they upset them too much. But now certain passages in *War and Peace* cause me such palpitations that I have to stop reading. When I read the passage describing the shooting of prisoners after the taking of Moscow by Napoleon I had to be sick. But all I got up was greenish bile.

I kept feeling my pulse and waited impatiently for the time when it would at last be irregular. Nothing of the kind. Frequent attacks of giddiness and physical weakness—that was all after six days without food. The craving for food did not diminish, but increased. I remember reading descriptions of how starving men gradually get a pleasant sensation of weightlessness and utter lightness. All bunk.

Sunday, April 11th.

Since for the moment I am unable to go on reading the bloodthirsty Tolstoy, I have started making up crossword puzzles. It is much more amusing, but also much more difficult than solving them. From one combination I got "Eumene." This certainly means something, but what? . . .

. . . I was still puzzling over "Eumene" when the Governor sent for me. He said he would try "to get my case expedited." He said that I looked seedy, and asked if I were ill. I replied that I had chronic heart trouble, but that it would certainly improve. He said he would try to get permission for me to be allowed into the fresh air now and again. I said that I should like nothing better.

The Governor also looked seedy and I asked him how his operation had gone. He said he was still very weak and that the best thing he could do would be to get himself prescribed a rest cure in a cell. Everyone laughed. When I got back to my cell I felt quite cheerful.

Then came Mass, accompanied by choral singing. The singing—the first music except for "Ya la-ee-la," which is not music at all, but rhythmical moaning—stirred me thoroughly.

But my pulse remained obstinately between eighty and eighty-eight, although a whole week had gone by.

Monday, April 12th.

A day of great, world-shaking events. . . .

First of all, I was shaved. During this operation a new warder was on duty—a youth in Phalangist uniform, with pince-nez, whom I had seen yesterday strutting about like a turkey-cock in the patio and bullying one or two wretched peasants. When the shaving was over, he stayed in my cell and went on with our conversation. Later Don Ramón and the librarian joined us, and it became a regular tea-party.

The youth in pince-nez indulged at intervals in charming witticisms, brandishing his revolver right under my nose and saying that sooner or later I would be shot, anyway. Don Ramón, who was sitting behind him on the bed, signed to me not to take him seriously, and even went so far as to tap his forehead. "If you were in my place and I were the warder," I said, or something like it, "you would find such jokes exceedingly distasteful." "That's true," he said, astonished, and from then on mended his manners somewhat. He abused the "Reds," and said they tortured their prisoners, put out their eyes, etc. I said that was absolutely untrue; I had imagined the same of the opposite side; one always thought the worst of the enemy. He said that also was true, and then added, with a grin: "Here in prison you're all treated like gentlemen, until you're shot; but if one of you falls into the hands of the Moors at the front it's no laughing matter, I can tell you."

I asked him whether, as a Catholic, he approved of the torturing of human beings. "Well, no," he said with an embarrassed smile. And so it went on for a while; in-between-times we talked about England, about Darwin, and whether men would ever fly to the moon.

This visit lasted nearly two hours. I wondered what it could all mean.

Then the mysterious librarian told me his story. He was not a professional boxer at all, but the proprietor of an advertising agency in Paris. Shortly before the outbreak of the Civil War he had gone bankrupt and had fled to Spain. His creditors had got on his tracks, and the French Government had requested the Spanish Government to arrest and extradite him. He was arrested in Seville a week before the Insurrection. The librarian —we will call him "Henri"—appealed against his extradition. Then the Civil War had begun, conditions in prison "had undergone certain changes," as he discreetly put it, and now it was Henri's dearest wish to be handed over to the authorities of his own country. All the more so since his creditors, touched by his dramatic story, had declared themselves ready to compound. The French Consul in Seville had done his best to get the lost sheep sent home again, but now the rebel authorities were unwilling to let him go. To them a Frenchman is a "Red," and the place for a "Red" is the prison patio. The ludicrous thing is that Henri alleges that he is a member of the "Croix de Feu," Colonel de la Rocque's Fascist organization.

Henri told his story with an air of injured innocence, and we kept having to laugh, Don Ramón, the youth with pince-nez, Henri and I. The two warders must have known the story inside out, for they nodded benevolently at every sentence as though listening to a well-worn anecdote. When he had finished the Phalangist declared that Henri too would be shot sooner or later; and then the tea-party broke up. As I saw my guests to the door, Don Ramón beckoned with his finger and allowed me to get a glimpse of the outside of my cell door.

I had been given a new plate; my name was on it—but "*Ojo*" and "*Incomunicado*" had vanished.

So this was the solution of the mystery. My solitary confinement, thanks to the good offices of the Governor, was at an end.

Round about seven the Phalangist returned, and informed me officially that from to-morrow morning onwards I was to be allowed to walk in the patio during the siesta hours, from one to three. I asked if I might now at last write to the Consul. He said "Yes," but letters must be written in ink and I could not buy pen and ink until to-morrow, as the canteen was closed.

Eureka!

I could now have started eating again, for my goal had been attained independently of my efforts. But out of caution I decided to wait until the letter to the Consul had been safely dispatched.

Monday night.

A moment ago—10 p.m.—the *jefe de servicio* was here. A *jefe* that I have never seen before, an elderly man with grizzled hair. He said that the office had received instructions from the military authorities that from to-morrow on I was to be allowed in the patio with the other prisoners, that is to say, the whole day long. Better still!

Tuesday, April 13th.

I was up by six and I waited in a fever of impatience for the moment when I should at last emerge from my hole. The prisoners appeared in the courtyard at 8 o'clock as usual—but my cell door was not opened. I drummed on the door—in vain. At last, at breakfast, the warder explained that a different *jefe* was was on duty to-day—"Scarface" of the leaking cistern incident—and that he said he had received no instructions with regard to me. I asked for pen and ink—this too was refused, "since the *jefe* had no instructions." I asked to speak to the *jefe*. He sent a message to say he was too busy.

I was about to fly into a towering rage.

. . . But I reflected that fortunately I had not broken my fast; that to-day was the ninth day; that my pulse—at last—varied between sixty and a hundred-and-five, and that it could be only a few more days at the most before they would have to transfer me to a hospital.

Tuesday evening.

At 12 o'clock Angelito suddenly came in with a message from the *jefe* to say that the military authorities had phoned through confirming that I was definitely to be allowed out in the patio between one and three . . . he had received no instructions, however, to let me have pen and ink.

A fresh period of feverish waiting until one. At last the

whistle sounds, the prisoners in the patio line up four abreast and are led indoors. The patio is empty. In ten minutes' time, at the most, Byron, the consumptive, Carlos and the newcomer must appear; and then at last my cell door will be opened. . . . A quarter-past one comes, half-past one, a quarter to two, nothing stirs. The others do not appear in the patio either.

I cannot contain myself any longer and I start beating out a tattoo on the door—hammer with my tin bowl on the steel and kick it till my feet are sore. It makes a hell of a din. After two minutes of this the door opens and Angelito, the *jefe* and "Captain Bligh" appear. They storm at me in chorus; Angelito loudest of all. (He has not had a tip for the last few days and knows that I have only twenty pesetas left.) I explain why I have been drumming on the door. "Captain Bligh" thunders that he will let me out when it suits him, and if it doesn't suit him he won't let me out at all; and if I behave like this again he will stamp on me, trample on me, crush me like a worm.

All this takes place in the open doorway. Byron, the consumptive and the newcomer, who have obviously just been let out of their cells, stand listening in the corridor. Then we are all four allowed out into the courtyard.

I feel the hot sun on my face, inhale a mouthful of air—and then everything suddenly turns grey, green, black before my eyes, and I find myself sitting on the ground. The other three set me on my legs again. Byron and the newcomer grasp me under the armpits; and after a few steps I am all right again.

We stand about together in a group, opposite Cell 36. At first I can do nothing but breathe in the air. Real air again for the first time—instead of the dense gaseous mixture, compounded of the odour of the stuffy bed, the smell of stale food and the stench of the lavatory on which I have existed for the past two months. Then we start talking.

My first question is, of course, what sentences they have been given.

"*La muerte*—death," says Byron, and grins.

"*La muerte*," says the consumptive. He is a well-known Republican politician, and Byron was formerly his secretary; they have both been waiting for three months to be shot.

"*La muerte*," says the third man. He is a little Andalusian peasant, a Militiaman, taken prisoner on the Almería front.

Carlos was not there; presumably he is ill.

Carlos is an Italian, a lieutenant in the Italian contingent fighting under Franco's leadership. His arrest seems to be somehow connected with his German friend.

The Militiaman is called Nicolás. He was taken prisoner ten days ago and sentenced three days ago. He was charged, as are all prisoners of war, with "*rebelión militar*"—armed rebellion. Nicolás told us, as we paced up and down the patio, of his trial by the Seville court-martial.

It had lasted three minutes. The President had read out the prisoner's name, birthplace and the name of the place where he was captured. The Prosecutor had demanded the death penalty, and had added: "I only regret that I cannot send this *rojecillo*—this miserable little Red—in a cage to Geneva before he is shot, in order to show the League of Nations what pitiable objects are these so-called fighters for justice and democracy."

Then they had marched him off.

Nicolás had somehow managed to get hold of a stalk of lettuce; he nibbled away at it as he told us his story, and offered us each a leaf. I refused—thinking of my heart; the two others accepted with alacrity. "When do you think they'll shoot me?" asked Nicolás. "*Paciencia*, my boy," said the Republicans with all the contempt of old inmates for the greenhorn. "One must not expect too much. We've been waiting three months now."

But then we all three began to comfort him. He was more afraid, even, than we were, for the ink was scarcely dry on his death sentence. We told him stories about how death sentences were only passed as a joke, to frighten people, and actually no one was ever shot; we three, who had been in prison an aggregate of eight months, and were not dead yet, were living proofs of this. He was only too glad to believe it, and in the end we believed it ourselves. We became quite gay, and Byron suggested that a notice should be hung in the patio between one and three:

"No admittance except to those showing death sentences."

I offered to lend Nicolás a book, but he said that he could not read. He stroked the cover of the Tolstoy lovingly with his horny peasant's paws, and his eyes took on a stupid, sad look. He said he had hoped, once the war was won, to have an opportunity of learning to read.

To-morrow is the anniversary of the proclamation of the Spanish Republic. The consumptive and his secretary are racking their brains wondering what sort of flags the foreign consulates in Seville and Burgos will fly. From the tone of their discussion I gather that this argument has been going on for weeks; they share a cell. Little Nicolás enquired despondently if they had nothing better to worry about, whereupon Byron drew himself up like a Spanish hidalgo and flashed at him: "No, Señor."

The air smelt glorious; it smelt of spring and the sea.

We were not taken back to our cells until half-past three.

At seven o'clock Angelito arrived with pen and ink. I had given him a five-peseta voucher to change for me, but he forgot to return me the three pesetas change.

Wrote my letter to the British Consul in Seville, but hear that it cannot be posted till to-morrow morning. To-morrow when the letter has gone off, I rather think my heart will improve.

To-morrow will be the tenth day of my illness.

Wednesday, April 14th. (Anniversary of proclamation of the Spanish Republic.)

Gave letter to warder at breakfast-time, but he brought it back from the prison censor's office, saying that it must be written in Spanish. The merchant from Gibraltar who interpreted for me before was called in to help me to write it in correct Spanish. Afterwards he told me that he had come to Seville some weeks ago with a Spaniard on business in connection with the delivery of war material—whereupon they had both been arrested. There are three of them in No. 33; the third is the representative of a big American automobile firm, and he is also there for currency smuggling. They obtain food, wine and even coffee from the hotel, and in addition Angelito buys from forty to fifty pesetas' worth of goods for them every day in the canteen. They are the aristocrats of the prison; I hate them. The fellow promised to have some coffee and a chicken sent to my cell—am convinced he will not keep his promise. (P.S. I was right.)

He went on to say that he and his friends "hoped shortly to move into No. 39," just as though he were talking of rooms in an hotel. He said, further, that Angelito was a bloody bastard who would murder his own brother for a tip.

At midday my letter at last went off—I saw Don Antonio post it in the box in the corridor, after it had been censored. He says that the Consul is certain to come to-morrow.

A nauseating set-to with Angelito over the three pesetas. He said I could do what I liked with my beastly money, but again did not return it.

Then, shortly after one, pretty punctually this time, I was let out into the patio again. The two Republicans were there, and Carlos.

But Nicolás was missing.

I was about to ask the warder what had become of him, but

the other two urgently advised me not to. Carlos kept at a distance from us; he had cut a swastika out of paper and stuck it in his buttonhole, and he stumped up and down alone by the outer wall.

Finally I did ask the warder after all. He shrugged his shoulders and said nothing . . .

Requiescat in pace, Nicolás. Let us hope it was all over swiftly and that they did not make you suffer too much. They chose a solemn day for your execution. I wonder what flags the consulates flew?

Little you were, a little Andalusian peasant, with soft, slightly prominent eyes, one of the poor and humble; this book is dedicated to you. What good does it do you? You could not read it even if you were still alive. That is why they shot you: because you had the impudence to wish to learn to read. You and a few million like you, who seized your old firearms to defend the new order which might perhaps some day have taught you to read.

They call it armed rebellion, Nicolás. They call it the hand of Moscow, Nicolás. They call it the instinct of the rabble, Nicolás. That a man should want to learn to read.

My God, they should really have sent you to Geneva in a cage, with the inscription:

"Ecce Homo, Anno Domini 1937."

XVII

I HAD intended to stop my hunger strike as soon as my letter to the Consul had been sent off.

The letter had gone off just before I was allowed out into the patio. Then I learned of Nicolás' execution, and was so shattered by it that I postponed the celebration of my first meal until the next day.

This was Thursday, April 15th.

I breakfasted on coffee with extra condensed milk and cake from the canteen; it was exactly ten days since I had touched any food. But my pleasure was spoilt. At every bite I was reminded of the lettuce which Nicolás had offered me.

I could scarcely bear to wait till one o'clock to be let out into the courtyard. Carlos was there, complete with swastika. The two others were not there.

We walked up and down, Carlos and I, avoiding each other and, both of us very pale, keeping an eye on the door from which they should have appeared.

At last Carlos came up to me—hitherto we had not exchanged a single word—introduced himself formally as Lieutenant Carlos T., and said that early that morning through his spy-hole he had seen the two of them being marched down the corridor.

He didn't make any comment. Neither did I. We paced up and down the empty courtyard together in silence.

But a few seconds later the door opened and the two Republicans appeared, washed and shaved.

We were so overjoyed that we rushed up to them, and then we all shook hands and patted each other on the back. The two others explained that they had been taken to have a shower that morning. We said not a word to them of what we had feared; but they guessed it.

As a result of all this Carlos and I had suddenly become friends. We spoke German to each other, and he told me his story.

Carlos was a lieutenant in the Italian force. He had participated in the entry of the rebel forces into Malaga, and remembered marching past Sir Peter's house and noticing the Union Jack. He even fancied that he had seen me standing on the balcony. Later he had been sent to the Madrid front.

In the meantime, during a short leave at Seville, he had made friends with a German transport driver. The German, who was called Johnnie, was the blond young man I had seen in the courtyard.

Johnnie, it turned out later, was a bit of a rotter; had on several occasions got himself into trouble with the German police, and had finally volunteered for the German expeditionary corps in Spain, because he had heard that lots of money was to be made there. In the middle of March, at the request of the German authorities, Johnnie had been arrested in Seville, and Carlos had been recalled to Seville from the Madrid front to give evidence with regard to his friend. He had been summoned to appear at police headquarters. Arrived there, he had been so discourteously treated by the Civil Guards in the course of his examination that, feeling a slur had been cast on his honour as an officer, he had punched the Chief of Police in the nose. Whereupon they had handcuffed him—and here he was now in prison.

The most curious thing in the whole of this curious story was that Carlos should have been put with us condemned prisoners. Probably because the authorities did not want to put him with Johnnie. Moreover, they did not dare to herd him, as an Italian officer, with the criminals in the "beautiful patio"; so here he was with us.

This was what we surmised. But Carlos confessed to me that he found our company extremely disquieting. He was very much afraid that they would come for him one night and shoot him out of hand. I told him that was nonsense and that his case was bound to be cleared up in a few days.

He said that if I had any idea of what went on between the Spaniards and Italians I would not talk so optimistically. The fact that an Italian officer could be marched off in handcuffs spoke volumes for the idyllic relations existing between them. He had come to Spain out of sheer enthusiasm (incidentally his pay was four thousand lire a month, plus forty pesetas a day expenses allowance); and now they'd gone and put him into jug like a common criminal, and taken away his money and papers. He had nothing to smoke, no comb, no soap, nothing to read. . . .

I said that he needn't bother to go on with the catalogue, I knew all about it. I found the young man distinctly charming, but was unable to suppress a certain feeling of malicious pleasure at his discomfiture.

He was twenty-two years old, a naturalized Italian of Austrian origin, and a student in Milan. He was studying to become a Latin teacher in a secondary school.

He was wearing the swastika because the fasces were too difficult to cut out of paper.

He said he had been convinced that those fighting on the side of the Reds were mostly Russians, and had been amazed to find so many Spaniards on the other side.

He said he had been convinced that all Reds were barbarians and that he was surprised to find what nice people the two Republicans and I were.

Carlos's character was a touching mixture of naïveté, narrow-mindedness and good-natured ambition to get on in this complicated world. But this, apparently, he was not finding so easy.

I had spent the first two months in the Seville prison in complete isolation. Only now, when I came into contact with the other prisoners, did I learn what was going on around me.

I learned that in the week after my transfer to the prison thirty-seven men from the big patio had been executed.

In the last week of February no executions had taken place; in March, forty-five.

Most of the victims were prisoners of war from the various fronts. In every case the procedure had been the same as in that of Nicolás.

True, not a single man had been shot without trial. But these trials were far more disgraceful than the unceremonious slaughter of prisoners in the front lines, immediately after a battle.

In the case of every single prisoner of war, without exception, the charge was one of "rebelión militar." Those who were defending the legal Government against open rebellion, were condemned for taking part in a rebellion—by an authority that claimed to be a court of law and to pronounce judgment in the name of justice.

The scenario of this sinister comedy was always the same. The proceedings lasted two or three minutes. The so-called Prosecutor demanded the death sentence; always and without exception. The so-called Defending Officer—always and without exception—asked for a life sentence in view of mitigating circumstances. Then the prisoner was marched off. He was never informed of his sentence. Sentence was passed the moment he was out of the door; it was one of death; always and without exception.

The record of the sentence was passed on to the Commander-in-Chief of the Southern Forces, General Queipo de Llano. The sentences were carried out in summary fashion. Twenty to twenty-five per cent of the prisoners—according to Queipo's mood or the situation at the front—were reprieved. The rest were shot.

Theoretically, the final decision lay with General Franco. In a few cases—especially if there were a risk of international repercussions—the Generalissimo granted a commutation. As for the *pobres y humildes*, he never even saw the lists of those condemned. Nicolás, for instance, had been shot on the fourth day after his trial; it is technically impossible that in such a short time his dossier should have travelled from the Court to Queipo, from Queipo to Franco's H.Q. in Salamanca or Burgos, and then back again.

From the moment he left the court-martial the accused was kept in uncertainty as to his fate. Were his sentence commuted to thirty years' imprisonment he was informed by letter—a week or a month or six months later. Were the death sentence confirmed, he learned of it only at the moment of execution.

In the interval he was left to play football and leap-frog in the patio, and count his buttons every morning to see whether he were going to be shot that night.

There were men in the patio who had been waiting for four months to be shot. The record was held by a Captain of the Militia—four and a half months. He was executed a few days before my release.

Nicolás had been lucky; he had had to wait only four days.

During March forty-five men were shot.

During the first thirteen days of April there were no executions.

During the night of April 13th to 14th seventeen men were shot, in celebration of the anniversary of the proclamation of the Republic. Nicolás was among them.

Two nights later, the night of Thursday, eight were shot. This was the first time I heard anything.

The proceedings were very subdued; perhaps that explains why I hadn't heard them before. But now I was on the watch.

I had learned that the critical time was between midnight and two o'clock in the morning. For some days I stood from midnight until two o'clock with my ear pressed to the door of my cell.

During the first night of my vigil, the night of Wednesday, nothing happened.

During the second night . . .

A feeling of nausea still comes over me when I remember that night.

I had gone to sleep, and I woke up shortly before midnight. In the black silence of the prison, charged with the nightmarish dreams of thirteen hundred sleeping men, I heard the murmured prayer of the priest and the ringing of the sanctus bell.

Then a cell door, the third to the left of mine, was opened, and a name was called out. "*Qué?*"—What is the matter?— asked a sleepy voice, and the priest's voice grew clearer and the bell rang louder.

And now the drowsy man in his cell understood. At first he only groaned; then in a dull voice, he called for help: "*Socorro, socorro.*"

"*Hombre,* there's no help for you," said the warder who accompanied the priest. He said this neither in a hostile nor in a friendly tone; it was simply a statement of fact. For a moment the man who was about to die was silent; the warder's quiet, sober manner puzzled him. And then he began to laugh. He kept slapping his knees with his hands, and his laughter was quiet and subdued, full of little gasps and hiccoughs. "You are only pretending," he said to the priest. "I knew at once that you were only pretending."

"*Hombre,* this is no pretence," said the warder in the same dry tone as before.

They marched him off.

I heard him shouting outside. But the sound of the shots came only a few minutes later.

In the meantime the priest and the warder had opened the door of the next cell; it was No. 42, the second to my left. Again, "*Qué?*" And again the prayer and the bell. This one sobbed and whimpered like a child. Then he cried out for his mother: "*Madre, madre!*"

And again: "*Madre, madre!*"

"*Hombre,* why didn't you think of her before?" said the warder.

They marched him off.

They went on to the next cell. When my neighbour was called, he said nothing. Most probably he was already awake, and, like me, prepared. But when the priest had ended his prayer, he asked, as if of himself: "Why must I die?" The priest answered in five words, uttered in a solemn voice but rather hurriedly: "Faith, man. Death means release."

They marched him off.

They came to my cell and the priest fumbled at the bolt. I could see him through the spy-hole. He was a little, black, greasy man.

"No, not this one," said the warder.

They went on to the next cell. He, too, was prepared. He asked no questions. While the priest prayed, he began in a low voice to sing the "Marseillaise." But after a few bars his voice broke, and he too sobbed.

They marched him off.

And then there was silence again.

And now I realized why the merchant from Gibraltar had said that he and his friends would shortly be moving in to No. 39.

I frequently awoke during this night feeling my bed shaking, as though in an earthquake. Then I realized that it was my own body that was trembling from head to foot. The moment I awoke my body grew still; the moment I fell asleep the nervous trembling began again. I thought at first that it was a permanent affliction like shell shock: but I only had two further attacks in the next few days; then it passed off. Carlos was in a far worse plight. He had heard all that I had heard. During the night of Friday, nine were shot; during Saturday night, thirteen. We heard everything, four nights running. On Monday morning I was called to Carlos's cell; he was lying on the ground by the door, foam on his lips, both legs stiff and paralysed.

In the space of five days they had shot forty-seven men. Even for this prison it was a record. The faces in the patio were grey; during a game of football two men had a set-to and pulled each other's hair out in handfuls. In the morning the warders who had been on night duty crept along the corridors, pale, scared, and troubled. Even Angelito, who had to open the doors of the condemned cells night after night, arrived one morning red-eyed. "If this goes on," he said, "they'll finish us all off."

Our two Republicans in the siesta patio carried it off best. Once, on Sunday, when we looked up at the window of one of the mass cells, from which one of their friends used to wave through the iron bars at three each afternoon, his cell companions signalled back that his turn had come the night before. Whereupon Byron had to vomit; then he lit a cigarette and uttered an obscenity.

When we were marched back to our cells, we did not dare, out of superstition, to say "*hasta mañana*" (until to-morrow). We murmured "*hasta* . . ." and were ashamed of being so superstitious.

One evening Don Antonio came back into my cell after serving out the food. "Why are you eating so little?" he asked. I said I had no appetite. "Are you afraid?" he asked. I reflected for a while and then said "Yes." He did not reply but, shrugging his shoulders, offered me a cigarette and pulled the door carefully to, without slamming it.

Carlos told me that two had been taken from Johnnie's cell the night before. Johnnie had told him that they had both wept and he had cracked jokes about the cowardice of the Reds. Carlos had asked Johnnie whether he himself was not afraid. Johnnie said that he wasn't a lousy Red. One of the executed Reds had lent him two pesetas the day before; at least he wouldn't have to return the money now.

I asked Carlos whether he proposed to go on being friends with Johnnie. He said he would like to strangle him with his bare hands.

We had become very free with such expressions. Death stalked the prison; we felt the beating of his wings, he buzzed round our faces like a tiresome fly. Wherever we went, wherever we stood, we could not get rid of that buzzing.

During the night of Saturday I again heard laughter—like that that had come from No. 43.

It was pretty infectious, and I wonder things went off so smoothly.

On Sunday, while I was in the patio, a head was poked out of a window of one of the mass cells on the second floor—these windows had no bars in front of them. The owner of the face had a black cap perched on an ugly little head, and looked like a jockey. He shouted down to us, asking whether any of us knew Hungarian.

I am of Hungarian origin; the fact must have got round in the prison.

The man called out to me in Hungarian that he had got a letter the day before telling him that he would be shot within the next two days. If ever I got back to Hungary, would I let his family know?

I said it was nonsense; no one was ever told before being shot.

While talking to the Hungarian, I did not dare to look upwards; we stood opposite each other, Byron and I, and gesticulated silently so that the head warder, when looking out of the window, might think we were talking to one another.

The Hungarian replied that, not knowing Spanish, he had been unable to read the letter, but his cell companions had told him that it contained the information that he was to be shot. Then he went on to say that thirty-five had been taken out of the adjoining mass cell during the past month.

I asked him where.

"Don't ask such a stupid question," he said. "Where all Spaniards are taken—to the butcher's block."

The Hungarian was still there the next day. He threw me down a letter for his wife. I did not dare to look up at him; I had been warned that there were men in the barber's shop, the windows of which also looked on to the patio, who blabbed everything they saw to the head warder.

During the next few days notes were frequently thrown out to me from cell windows, warning me of spies. Some of them warned me of Carlos, whose swastika had attracted everyone's notice. "Take care, foreigner," one of the notes ran. "There are spies here who are anxious to save their own lives by handing others over to the executioner."

The notes were either rolled up into little balls or else tied up with a bit of string. When we saw a note fall at the other end of the courtyard, two of us strolled over, came to a halt, went on talking, and finally let a cigarette or a book fall to the ground so as to be able to pick up the note without being detected. Then we unfolded the note in our trousers' pockets and put it away in the book. Finally Byron or I sat down with our backs to the wall and read—apparently the book, in reality the note.

The next day the Hungarian was still there. He threw me down a fresh letter of farewell to his wife.

For five days running his head appeared at the window on

the stroke of two and a fresh letter of farewell was dropped into the courtyard. On the sixth day one of his cell companions appeared behind him, pulled a face and tapped his forehead. Something began to dawn on us.

In the end we learned the solution of the riddle through Carlos, who had got it from Johnnie. The Hungarian was a volunteer in Franco's Foreign Legion and was in prison because of some fraud or other. His cell contained five Republican Militiamen who were condemned to death. It wasn't exactly an elevating experience for them to have to share a cell with an enemy. Particularly the most detested kind of enemy, a foreign mercenary; and to have to be marched off to death before his eyes. The Hungarian didn't know any Spanish. One day, when he received an official communication, they tricked him into believing that he was going to be shot. They wanted to have the satisfaction of knowing that he also should feel what death tasted like. After a week the two survivors out of the five were fed up with his moaning and explained it all to him. Shortly afterwards he was released.

Should any moralist feel a need to comment on the matter, I should like to say that I regard the conduct of the Militiamen as completely reprehensible and that in their place I should have behaved in exactly the same way.

On the night of Tuesday seventeen were shot.
On Thursday night eight.
On Friday night nine.
On Saturday night thirteen.
I tore strips off my shirt and stuffed my ears with them so as not to hear anything during the night. It was no good. I cut my gums with a splinter of glass, and said they were bleeding, so as to obtain some iodized cotton wool. I stuffed the cotton wool in my ears; it was no good, either.

Our hearing became preternaturally sharp. We heard everything. On the nights of the executions we heard the telephone ring at ten o'clock. We heard the warder on duty answer it. We heard him repeating at short intervals: "ditto . . ، ditto . . . ditto. . . ." We knew it was someone at military headquarters reading out the list of those to be shot during the night. We knew that the warder wrote down a name before every "ditto." But we did not know what names they were and we did not know whether ours was among them.

The telephone always rang at ten. Then until midnight or one o'clock there was time to lie on one's bed and wait. Each night we weighed our lives in the balance and each night found them wanting.

Then at twelve or one we heard the shrill sound of the night bell. It was the priest and the firing squad. They always arrived together.

Then began the opening of doors, the ringing of the sanctus bell, the praying of the priest, the cries for help and the shouts of "Mother."

The steps came nearer down the corridor, receded, came nearer, receded. Now they were at the next cell; now they were in the other wing; now they were coming back. Clearest of all was always the priest's voice: "Lord, have mercy on this man, Lord, forgive him his sins, Amen." We lay on our beds and our teeth chattered.

On Tuesday night seventeen were shot.

On Thursday night eight were shot.

On Friday night nine were shot.

On Saturday night thirteen were shot.

Six days shalt thou labour, saith the Lord, and on the seventh day, the Sabbath, thou shalt do no manner of work.

On Sunday night three were shot.

XVIII

Monday, April 19th.

Hitherto I have always been shaved in my cell; yesterday they took me to the barber's shop. Saw myself in a mirror for the first time for two and a half months. Was astonished to find myself so unchanged. A man is really as elastic as a football; you get a kick which you imagine will knock you to pieces; but the outer case springs back into shape and the only trace left is at the most a spattering of mud. If our consciousness were the aggregate of our experiences we should all be grey at twenty-five.

The water-pipe that runs through my cell sometimes acts like a speaking-tube. If I lay my ear to it, I can hear confused noises: now a few bars of wireless music coming from the Governor's room, now a jumble of noises from several cells. Sometimes I even think I can hear women's voices—the wing on the other side is the women's prison. For the last three days all these sounds from distant spheres have been drowned by the voice of one man who keeps sobbing and crying for his mother. He must be in one of the cells near mine. Whenever I put my ear to the pipe I can hear him. I asked Angel who it was that was continually crying. He said it was a Militia-man who had formerly shared the cell with his brother, but who since Friday night had been alone.

This morning, after they had taken breakfast round, the warder and Angel came back into my cell. "Come quickly," said the warder. "Your friend has gone off his head." We went to Cell 37. On the floor, parallel with the iron bedstead, lay Carlos, stretched out at full length, the swastika still in his buttonhole. The sweat was pouring down his face, and little bubbles of foam had formed on his lips. His eyes were wide open. I looked at him, and did not know what to think. The warder dug me in the ribs. "Go on, say something to him," he said. "Talk German to him." (Carlos spoke only a few broken words of Spanish, and I had already interpreted for him several times.)

I asked Carlos what the devil was the matter with him; I shook him, I pinched his arm—he did not show the slightest reaction and did not seem to know me. Angel and I fetched a bucket of water and poured it over his head. Then we pulled his ears. After this he gradually came to, and began to whimper and wave his hands about. We held him down and I talked to him until at last he recognized me and began inconsequentially to complain that his back hurt him and that he could not move his legs. We felt his legs; they were as stiff as pokers and the knees would not bend. When we tried to bend them by force, he roared with pain.

Finally we laid him on the bed, and the doctor's assistant—one of the prisoners, a medical student—came along. We diagnosed the case as hysteria. Then the *jefe de servicio* arrived and said that it was nothing but malingering, and that if we took no notice of Carlos, he would soon pull himself together.

At last they all went out of the cell and left me alone with Carlos. I did not turn my head, but I was certain that the *jefe* was peeping through the spy-hole.

I said to Carlos that if he were malingering he might safely tell me; I certainly wouldn't peach on him. But he did not understand me and all that I could get out of him was that he had been hearing the same sounds as I myself at night, that the priest with the sanctus bell had approached his cell; he had heard the tinkle of the bell growing louder and louder and had known no more. . . .

After a few minutes they came for me and locked me in

my own cell again. The *jefe* said that if Carlos was not better by midday he would be put in a punishment cell, and that would certainly cure him.

Poor Carlos. His legs were cleverer than his head; when he thought he was about to go to his death they stiffened and refused to carry him.

If he is left a cripple, they will pin no medal on his breast.

Only three of us in the patio this afternoon. I told Byron and the consumptive the whole story; they shrugged their shoulders and did not seem to be particularly moved. But afterwards they gave Angel some cigarettes to take to Carlos in his cell.

At the evening meal I asked the warder how Carlos was. He merely tapped his forehead and said, "Your *amigo* is balmy."

Wrote a fresh letter to the Consul. The first was sent off five days ago. Since when I have been daily and hourly expecting a visit from him, or at least an answer. Am convinced that the first letter must have gone astray; otherwise inexplicable that he should not have responded within twenty-four hours to my S O S.

It is a dreadful disappointment. For two and a half months I fought for permission to write the letter—for ten days I have had "heart attacks"—and now there's no answer, nothing.

Tuesday, April 20th.

Nothing from Consul.

But the first quiet night for days.

No telephone in the evening. No night-bell.

I feel like a convalescent. The whole prison seems to breathe again.

In the morning I was called to Carlos once more. Yesterday evening he had been a little better, had eaten something and tried to hobble round the room on his stiff legs. Now he is unconscious again. While I was in his cell a representative came from the Italian Consulate to take a record of the whole case. But Carlos could not be made to come to. This is the clearest possible proof that he is not putting it on—he too has waited long enough to get into touch with his Consulate.

Wednesday, April 21st.

Yesterday, when the warder brought my evening meal, he said with marked kindliness that I must eat up, and ordered me a second helping. It seemed to me that Angel and the other orderly looked at me very peculiarly when the warder said this. Then the wine arrived, and, against the rules, I was given a second beakerful without my asking for it. The orderly who brought the wine also looked at me rather peculiarly, I thought.

I was convinced that my turn had come.

I did not go to sleep, but paced up and down, waiting for the telephone to ring, and was amazed at my own indifference. It occurred to me that I found it harder to part from Byron and the consumptive and Angel than from all my friends and relatives.

At ten o'clock sharp the telephone rang. Seven times I heard "Ditto—ditto—ditto."

I paced up and down until eleven; then I suddenly felt very tired. Surely, I thought, I may as well lie down for another hour. When I woke up they were bringing my breakfast.

I really do not understand how I managed it. I am more and more puzzled at the working of the wheels within my brain—I wonder, indeed, that they still work at all. I am convinced that Carlos has more physical courage than I—in Malaga he got a bayonet-wound in the arm in a hand-to-hand fight, and I had been much impressed by the way in which he had related the story. And now he lies there in the grip of a hysterical attack, and the rôles are reversed.

It's quite different for the two Spaniards. There are two of them at night. This makes an enormous difference.

But if the warder .and Angelito offer me a second helping again, I shall bash their faces in.

Or was it, after all, not imagination, and had they perhaps known of an order which was only cancelled at the last moment?

I shall never know.

No news again from the Consul.

Thursday, April 22nd.

Late last evening letter from Consul arrived. Dated 20th. Writes that he has received my letters of the 14th and 19th and has requested to be allowed to visit me.

Once more granite rocks have turned out to be air-balloons.

Was at first mad with delight—then overcome by nausea at finding myself so indifferent to the fate of the others, now that I felt comparatively safe. This feeling of nausea was so intense that I could not sleep, although to-night all was still. Strange how all happy events—the letter from home, the money, the letter from the Consul—all turn back on one. The urge to bear the burden of the others acts on me like a categorical imperative; and it is, after all, merely a question of taste that I say "burden" instead of "cross."

But from the same source comes the equally ardent desire to slay the greasy little black priest who rings the sanctus bell at nights.

Carlos was better to-day; he stumped about with us in the courtyard. His legs are still somewhat stiff, but that will probably soon pass off.

The Spaniards, on the other hand, were in a great state. They came into the courtyard, oddly agitated, and fell upon me, both at once, demanding to know which was the better newspaper, *The Times* or the *Daily Herald*. I realized that they must have had a bitter quarrel on the subject and so I tried to frame my answer in a manner worthy of Solomon. This was the worst thing I could have done, for then each maintained that he was right and they lost their heads completely and screamed at each other. It would not have taken much for them to have gone for one another's throats.

Our patio more and more resembles a panopticon—Carlos with his paralysed legs, the other two with their nervous irritability and quarrelsomeness, and I with my insane qualms of conscience and mental purification rites after the Dominican model.

.... Is this to be taken *cum grano salis?* I myself no longer know.

Friday, April 23rd.

At three o'clock, when we were led back from the patio, I was given permission to go to the canteen myself to spend my last few pesetas on cigarettes. Johnnie was standing in the canteen drinking coffee. He looked as though he were going to speak to me, but I turned my back on him.

Then came Henri, the librarian. He was in radiant mood and told me that to-morrow at last he was being sent back to France. Promised me to go and see my wife in London or write to her.

(P.S. He did neither, of course.)

The comparative freedom of movement that I now enjoy makes the periods of being alone almost harder to bear. When, at three o'clock, the cell door falls to behind me, the waiting for the next afternoon begins.

The Consul has not been yet. What if they refuse to allow him to come at all?

Saturday, April 24th.

Yesterday evening young Caballero came into my cell, accompanied by a warder. He is a nice boy of twenty-five or twenty-six, perhaps even younger, dressed in brown overalls. He is guarded specially strictly, and has been "*incomunicado*" without intermission for nearly a year; may speak to no one, is not allowed out in the patio, but only to march up and down the corridor for two hours daily, accompanied by a warder. I have often seen him through the spy-hole; he is always clean, tidy, and well-groomed, and apparently in good spirits. And yet he has had the same nightly experiences as I— and what he must have been through during the first few months, when a hundred, two hundred, three hundred, were marched off to execution every night, at that time without a trial or any kind of formality. . . .

Either the boy has a simple, childlike nature or else he is marvellously tough; I can't decide which.

He is very popular with the warders. When he appeared in my cell yesterday the warder explained that we might not talk to one another, and that they had merely come because Caballerito had nothing to read and had heard that I had the first volume of *War and Peace*. Had I perhaps finished it, or in any case would I lend it to Caballerito for one night?

I gave him the book and asked if I might be allowed to shake Caballerito by the hand. We smiled at each other and as we shook hands I saw that the boy's eyes were moist. Then they both marched off with the Tolstoy.

Early to-day the new librarian came. A political prisoner this time, a man of about thirty, a former Socialist town councillor from Galicia. He brought the second volume of Tolstoy and wanted the first returned. I said it was with Caballero. Whereupon he flared up and said we had no right to exchange books without his permission—he had sixteen hundred books to look after, where would he be, etc., etc. I said that a night without anything to read was worse than hell; that he as a political prisoner ought to know that perfectly well; that the situation of all of us was not, God knew, one for bureaucratic formalities and that the exchange had been made with the warder's approval.

Whereupon he said that he didn't wish to argue with me and if I were undisciplined he would not bring me any books at all.

To which I replied he could go to blazes, adding a few

more unprintable remarks. If the warder had not placed himself between us, we should have come to blows.

The librarian loped off. I felt as relieved after the row as after a purifying storm. But in half an hour's time he came back and mutely placed two books on the bed; a biography of Cervantes and a novel by Pío Baroja.

He made a formal apology and we shook hands, with emotion. Odd fish.

In the patio Carlos told me he had been taken in the morning to the Italian consulate under escort of two Civil Guards. The Consul had merely shaken his head resignedly at his story and told him he guaranteed that he would be released in the next few days. Carlos said he had the impression that the Consul had to deal with a dozen such cases every day. At the prison gates he had met the Governor, who had said in astonishment: "I thought, Teniente, you were free already."

Of course he is terribly happy. He has existed the whole time on the money he has borrowed from us; now he promises us mountains of gold when he's free. He means to write Mussolini a letter saying that we three ought to be released. He has even read out a draft of the letter to us. It begins with an account of his student years, his career in the Fascio, his military rank and his warlike deeds in Spain. Then it goes on to say that he has become convinced that the Reds are not all criminals, but many of them misguided idealists; then follows a heart-rending description of us three and finally the hope is politely but emphatically expressed that the Duce will, as proof of his nobility of spirit, restore us to the arms of our loved ones.

I had to translate it all into Spanish, and we were tactful enough to keep deadly serious faces.

Carlos then told us that there had been a group of pretty girls standing at the prison gates, flirting with the sentries.

The general atmosphere of the prison is considerably better; the last three nights have been undisturbed and everyone hopes that a quieter period is coming again.

I still stuff cotton wool into my ears every evening, but I have worked out a new system for the night. I sleep only five and a half hours, from nine to half-past two, force myself to get up at three, and remain awake the whole day so as to be certain of being able to sleep during the critical hours. The hours till the morning are long—I have to pace up and down or read standing up so as not to fall asleep—but the method has proved efficacious and the mere consciousness that I can thus get the better of the nightmares gives me satisfaction and relative peace.

Sunday, April 25th.

Consul still not come. Carlos still not released. Byron has begun to write poetry and put Basque folk-tales into verse. He admires the Basques and despises the Andalusians. He loves talking in aphorisms and said to-day, twirling his little moustache: "Andalusia, my friend, is the scrotum of Africa, while the Basque country is the heart of Spain." I said it was a fine definition.

His chief, on the other hand, gives way increasingly to melancholia. Hitherto they have both had money, and been able to have enormous meals every day; hors d'œuvres variés, beef-steak with fried egg and salad, fruit, black coffee, a bottle of wine per head, and chicken three times a week. Angelito used to take them all this every day in a basket and had done very well out of it. They refused to save, and every day Byron would say that the only thing he was afraid of was that they might be shot before they had devoured their money's worth. Now their money has given out; I too have no more, Carlos never had any. We have jointly borrowed twenty pesetas from Angel on condition we return him thirty when we get some. Then I have borrowed another ten from the other orderly. So at least we all have cigarettes.

XIX

On the next day—Monday, April 26th—there are only three sentences in my diary: "Fainted during the night. Another heart attack. This time it's bend or break. ...."

This of course was another lie for the benefit of the censor. What had happened was that during the previous night, under the influence of a particularly horrible scene, I had decided to resume my fasting and obtain my transfer to the hospital at all costs. Life in prison is a constant repetition of the same situations, the same thoughts and schemes. One lives and thinks in a vicious circle. The mind is made giddy by it; there is no escape. There is no progress, even time does not move forward in a straight line; it reappears in the same form.

The following thing had happened on that night:

On Sunday afternoon a new prisoner had been brought in and was taken to my old cell, No. 41.

I saw them bring him in. He was very young, about fifteen or sixteen.

Captain Bligh was on duty that afternoon. It was Angel's day off, and the second orderly, Manuel, was taking his place. Manuel was a little degenerate cripple, with pronounced signs of water on the brain. Rumour had it that he was in prison for a life term for some sexual offence that had had a fatal outcome. We all felt a certain physical aversion to him.

Towards evening Manuel got drunk. The orderlies often do. When he brought round the evening meal he could scarcely stand upright on his rickety legs, and the whole cell reeked of liquor.

At nine I heard Captain Bligh walking down the corridor with Manuel. They came to a halt outside No. 41.

"They'll send for him to-night," said Captain Bligh.

Manuel answered in his high-pitched, tipsy, grotesque squeak:

"Funny he should have to die. The whole day he has been asking to be let out into the patio. Funny. . . ."

Whereupon the warder:

"*Rojo, rojo*,"–meaning: Never mind, it's only a Red. I think he, too, was drunk. He boomed forth the "*rojo, rojo*" in his deep, husky bass so that it sounded as though he were snoring.

At this moment the lad in No. 41 began to beat on the door with his fists; he must have heard it all. "I don't want to die," he shouted. "Mother, mother help. I don't want to die. Help, help. . . ."

The whole corridor echoed with the noise. The prison grew restive. From all the cells came confused, indistinct sounds.

The boy went on bellowing.

Captain Bligh and Manuel fetched him from his cell and carried him off somewhere to a special isolation cell. On the way the drunken orderly stumbled and fell with a clatter to the ground. Other warders came up and helped to take the boy off.

A little later–it was not yet ten–the priest walked down the corridor, probably to confess the boy. Then a warder called out for brandy.

At ten the telephone rang. Three times I heard "*lo mismo*" –ditto.

Shortly after ten Don Ramón came to my cell and said that if there was a shindy later on I was not to worry–one of the prisoners was ill and they were going to move him to hospital in the night.

Obviously they were afraid the boy would put up a fight when they took him off. As a rule everything went off quietly during the execution nights; the priest and warders had obviously worked out a technique for preventing scenes.

At half-past ten I heard subdued whispering, tittering, and very odd snuffling and smacking noises in the corridor.

I looked through the spy-hole.

In the empty, lighted corridor a scene was being enacted, strange as a hallucination; little Manuel and Captain Bligh were playing at "horses." Manuel was the horse, and had a string tied round him; Captain Bligh was holding the reins. They paraded like this up and down the whole length of the corridor; I could see them whenever they passed the line of vision of my spy-hole. The warder was holding a whip, he called out, "Gee up!" at every step and laid on with it. Manuel tittered, and whimpered with pain by turns. After having traversed the corridor three times, horse and driver went out into the empty patio. I could hear the crack of the whip and Manuel's whimpers. Then they came back.

This was about eleven. Then I fell asleep. Next day I heard that three prisoners had been executed shortly after midnight. The boy had not screamed. Perhaps they had made him drunk on the brandy.

It was after this night that I decided afresh not to touch any food, and also to try not to drink any water. I was convinced that this time the effects of starvation would be bound to make themselves felt sooner—it was ten days since I had begun to take food again, and before that I had fasted for exactly ten days; then there was the fact that I had cut down my hours of sleep and was smoking heavily. This time I was determined to hold out until, one way or another, I got out of this slaughter-house.

I drank nothing for seven days and ate nothing for fifteen, from April 25th to May 9th. I imagined that I was fighting for my life; but apparently it was ordained that all my efforts should be made ridiculous, for the second hunger strike proved in the event as superfluous as the first. I was released independently of any action on my part, and all my desperate efforts had been mere tilting against wind-mills.

Monday, April 26th.

Hungry the whole day.* This time much worse than the first time. Was summoned to the office this evening. Two well-fed gentlemen from the Press Department in Salamanca greeted me very courteously, and gave me another letter from my wife.

The contents are a little more revealing than those of the first letter. She writes that she "was astonished to find how many friends we have," and that she "not only hopes, but has a definite feeling that I shall not have to wait very long now for my release."

This last no doubt is only a pious wish, but the first indicates that a campaign of protest has been got going.

The letter had been forwarded to Salamanca through the mediation of the Archbishop of Westminster.

But it is evident from the letter that my wife, despite all efforts, has not succeeded in discovering where I am. What object can the Franco authorities have in concealing my whereabouts? One more reason for holding out now. In a fortnight at the most I shall be a wreck and they will have to take me to hospital.

The two gentlemen from the Press Department said I might write an answer to the letter, and discreetly suggested that I should write to say how well I was being treated. I had the impression that they would not forward the letter and were merely trying to get a statement out of me. I wrote: "Up till now I have been treated properly in prison and have nothing to complain of."

---

* In the meantime I had so perfected my code that I no longer needed to write "heart" for "stomach" and could write down practically everything I wanted.

They took the letter away with them, promising that it would be in my wife's hands within a week.

(*It never arrived, of course.*)

Tuesday, April 27th.

Endless rainy day. Carlos still here. Both Spaniards in a very bad humour ever since our money gave out. Quarrel the whole time. As a result of fasting I, too, have become irritable, but take care to keep a hold on myself.

Wednesday, April 28th.

The Consul came to-day.

He said the British Government were taking a friendly interest in my case and he had received instructions to do what he could for me. Questions had been put in the House of Commons. My wife had moved heaven and earth to obtain my release. The Foreign Office had enquired of Franco what charge had been preferred against me, but Franco had refused to answer on the ground that my case was still *sub judice*.

Sub judice is good. First they declare to me and the world that I have been sentenced to death by court-martial. Then all of a sudden my case is *sub judice*; and they haven't once brought me up for examination.

I don't know what to make of it all; the Consul also doesn't seem to know. I asked him whether Franco had given a formal assurance that I should not be shot. He said that to his knowledge no such assurance had been given so far. I don't even know whether this new turn of events with regard to my case being *sub judice* is favourable or not. Probably Franco finds the stir the case has caused disagreeable, and his people want to stage a formal trial to condemn me "correctly." They'll work up the material that I published with regard to the German pilots so that it will be sufficient to procure a sentence by court-martial.

In short, I'm no wiser than I was before.

What I fear most is lest Queipo should turn the whole thing into a question of prestige, possibly even in relation to Franco. Salamanca seems to have protected me against Queipo up till now; but I'm in Seville and not in Salamanca.

The Consul promised to come every week and to let me know the moment he had any news from the Foreign Office. I asked him for various little things: money, a chessboard, books—he promised to bring them next time. We talked for nearly an hour, in an office. On the way back to my cell the warder showed me the ordinary visitors' room.

It is a big hall with a kind of iron cage in the middle. The prisoners who are receiving visitors crouch on the ground in the cage. Round the cage is an empty space of about five paces deep; on the further side of this the wives of the prisoners squat on the ground and shout across at them. There are at least a hundred people in the room at a time. I couldn't understand how the couples ever managed to make each other hear amid the general hullabaloo. The visits last ten minutes. Each prisoner may be visited once a week.

Thursday, April 29th.

Racked my brains the whole day over what the Consul told me. Postulated all kinds of theories, but came to no conclusion.

While we were out in the patio we heard an explosion from the direction of the town. All the windows rattled and we saw, some miles away, an enormous column of smoke slowly rising upwards.

Later we heard from the warder that a shoe factory had blown up from some unexplained cause. All the hands, two hundred of them, dead.

It was the Phalangist with pince-nez who told us the story. He added the wise commentary: "You see, there were two hundred of 'em—and here you all make a devil of a fuss if we pot off five or six of you."

Then he added that the day after next was May 1st and would no doubt be "solemnly celebrated."

Friday, April 30th.

Pangs of hunger the whole time; thirst even worse. Feel ill and very wretched; my heart beats like a drum. Torrential rain. Carlos, who has learned that Johnnie has been released, is livid with rage. Yesterday he declared a hunger strike, but started eating again to-day—he said the smell of coffee so titillated his nostrils that he could not hold out.

The last few nights have been quiet. But we all dread May 1st.

Saturday, May 1st.

Thank God, the night was quiet.

This afternoon, while the four of us were walking about in the patio, three *Requetes* officers appeared in the doorway. Captain Bligh was conducting them; he pointed a finger at us, and was obviously explaining who we were. We felt like animals in a zoo. The officers riveted their gaze on us, postured like elegant dandies, and struck their riding boots with their whips. It was far the most humiliating experience I have been through so far, more humiliating, even, than being photographed in the street in Malaga.

Sunday, May 2nd.

This night, too, quiet.

I am considerably weaker. Felt too ill to go out into the patio; lay on my bed the whole day. Have grown very thin—arms and legs only skin and bone now, like those of a mummy. This evening couldn't stand the thirst any longer—had drunk nothing for a week—and drank a whole litre of wine which I had saved up. Result what might have been expected. In addition smoked thirty-two cigarettes to-day. If I can keep this up much longer, I shall be able to earn my living in future as a "fasting man" at a fair.

Monday, May 3rd.

The whole day in bed, except for one hour in the late afternoon. In the evening Angelito brought me a second blanket and a kind of pillow. Unable to read.

I think I'll soon be bad enough now to get myself taken before the doctor.

Tuesday, May 4th.

Last night they shot another eight.

I didn't hear anything of it myself; learned of it to-day through other channels.

Lie all day long on my bed, dozing.

Three days now since I was in the patio.

Wednesday, May 5th.

Late last night Carlos was transferred to my cell. A new batch of prisoners; the prison is overcrowded.

We were tremendously pleased and talked the whole night. I had to let Carlos into the secret of my "hunger strike," since he can see me getting rid of my food. From now on he will eat up my rations.

This morning we were both transferred to Cell 17.

It is situated on the other side of the corridor; the window looks out on to the "beautiful patio." When we looked out of the window for the first time this morning and caught sight of flower-beds and green trees, it all seemed like a fairy tale. The flowers and trees of course are not exactly impressive—the "beautiful patio" looks rather like one of the wretched parks in a working-class district. But the main thing is that the trees and flowers have *colours*. I became suddenly aware that we are all of us here living in a world made up of the two shades, black and grey, like the world of the film. To continue the analogy: the "beautiful patio" had the same effect on me as a coloured film, the sight of which only later on makes one aware of the monotony of the black and grey technique.

I made a little test to see whether it was only I who reacted so violently to these things, or whether my reaction was typical of prison existence. I said not a word to Carlos about my delight, but he began himself to say how marvellous the flowers and trees were and almost clapped his hands for joy like a child.

The move had taken so much out of me that I lay down on my bed again after it and could scarcely breathe. To-day is the eleventh day of fasting. My appearance has reached an almost theatrical degree of emaciation; Carlos will bear me out. The *jefe*—"Scarface"—made an inspection of the cell after breakfast and the sight of me at last had the desired effect. He had me taken before the doctor.

The doctor—a military doctor with the rank of Colonel and obviously a specialist at detecting malingering—asked me what was the matter with me. I said something about *angina pectoris* and two attacks. He listened to my heart; prescribed no smoking and milk instead of coffee—that was all.

Carlos was very disappointed at the meagre result. He said it wasn't worth fasting twenty-one days for that. Just wait, I said, we're not dead yet. We were both somewhat horror-struck at this ominous phrase.

Lucky that the two of us are here together. Thus no one can find out whether I smoke or not. Am now smoking a little less, twenty a day. After each cigarette the cardiac muscle beats out a tattoo.

The criminals in the patio are a curious bunch. Three murderers, five or six burglars, a real Sierra bandit—the rest swindlers and petty delinquents. They don't play football and don't dash about like the politicos; they are a sedate, serious lot. They despise the politicos and talk with no hint of pity of the executions. They live an ordered life, secure, unmenaced—an idyllic existence. We were able to talk to them through the window with perfect ease, there's no taboo line here. They all cursed the war—since it has begun things have become so uncomfortable in prison. They're quite nice to me, but they don't care for Carlos because he's an officer.

"Serves you right," one of them said, "if you had stayed at home and lived a nice sober existence, you wouldn't have been in jug."

Thursday, May 6th.

Yesterday they took away the electric bulbs from our cell. There is a shortage of electric bulbs in the prison and in the whole of Seville. The warder explained to us that he needed the bulbs for the cells of the "*incomunicados*" and "*ojos.*" "You," he said, "are well-behaved chaps; there's no need to keep an eye on you any longer."

We felt highly flattered. We now belong to the patrician class of the prison, the warders talk to us in intimate, familiar tones about their duties; we are members of the family.

That is the way to get on in life.

What luck that there are two of us now that there's no light. Carlos was furious at first when I woke him up at three in the morning and announced that we would now converse until breakfast-time. But ever since he has been able, like me, to sleep through the critical hours, he blesses my system.

Carlos still goes out into the patio from one to three o'clock; he is my liaison with the outer world. I hear from him that our two friends are in a very bad humour and are constantly at loggerheads. For months they have been stuck together like Siamese twins; in sleep, in waking, in the performance of the most intimate functions.

But there have been no executions for the last three nights.

Friday, May 7th.

Was taken to the doctor this morning for the second time. He shook his head as he looked at me and was furious, because my symptoms do not fit in with any of the forms of malingering known to him. Was chiefly irritated at my answering, each time he asked me how I felt in myself, that I felt perfectly well, that it was not at my request that I had been brought before him that he could not help me, since there was no drug that could cure *angina pectoris*. I thought that, in view of the unmistakable symptoms of my condition, the man would at least feel some alarm at the thought of his responsibility and put me in hospital. I really look quite fantastic—like a walking skeleton out of a Walt Disney cartoon. When I was taken across the corridor to visit the doctor, all eyes were turned on me in horror.

But I was out of luck. After long reflection the doctor told me to show him my tongue. It was as white as though I had dipped it in flour. This gave him a sudden inspiration.

"I knew it," he roared jubilantly to his assistants. "The man is drugging himself with ether."

I enquired with a grin where he imagined I could get hold of ether.

He said that doubtless the criminals smuggled it in to me through the window.

I fancy he had sent for my record and had come upon the part about the hypodermic syringe. And perhaps, too, the "women's stockings."

But the affair had very unpleasant consequences. Carlos and I were moved to Cell 30, which looks out on the big patio. Our mattresses and clothes were slashed about to see if any ether could be discovered. Conscious of my innocence, I began to protest more and more loudly, and Carlos backed me up. Finally I staged a fit of fury which, owing to the ragged state of my nerves, was only half put on. Half a dozen warders came running up and "Scarface" was green with rage; but none of them dared to touch us. I fancy this was due to the effect of Carlos's presence; the spirit of Mussolini hovers invisibly in the cell with arms spread out protectively.

Since they found nothing, they confined themselves to boarding up the window to prevent ether being smuggled in. Now we sit all day in the dark and sing "*Gaudeamus igitur*" and Austrian student songs—we both studied for a term or two at Vienna University.

I apologized to Carlos for involving him in this mess, but he said that the affair was just beginning to amuse him.

Besides, he gets double rations.

While he eats I wrap my head in the blanket so as not to hear or see anything of it. To-day is the thirteenth day.

Carlos is a boon. I do not know how I should have borne the last few days without him.

He has cut out a fresh swastika from cigarette-paper and the rebel flag from a match-box cover and wears them both together in his button-hole.

Saturday, May 8th.

I was brought up for examination for the first time.

At one o'clock, when Carlos had gone out into the patio, I dozed off with weakness. This was in contravention of my iron rule as regards sleep, but I am now so weak that I fall asleep without realizing it as I sit, sometimes even in the midst of talking.

At half-past one I was awakened by the opening of the cell door. The "*Venga*"—come—rang out in more cold, official tones than I had heard for a long time.

They took me to the office. In the office were an officer and a uniformed shorthand typist. My greeting was ignored and I was not offered a seat.

I knew at once that this was the military examiner. I had visualized this scene for long enough beforehand.

I said that I was ill and must sit down; that I would refuse to answer any questions until they brought me a chair. The officer shrugged his shoulders and had a chair brought in. He had a thick file of documents before him; while he was opening it I managed to read the inscription on the cover; my name, and, in brackets, the offence with which I was charged. "*Auxilio de rebelión militar,*" it read.

For "affording aid to armed rebellion" there was, I knew, only one possible sentence before Franco's courts-martial: death. Nevertheless I felt relieved. The fact that they had on their own initiative dropped the charge of spying seemed to me a favourable omen.

The examination lasted some two hours. Almost half an hour of this was taken up by the examiner in trying to get me to admit that the *News Chronicle* was a Communist paper. The man's ignorance was astounding. He was convinced that a paper which took up a loyal attitude to the legal Spanish Government was bound to be Communist. The examination developed into an argument. Then, when he realized that he was giving himself away, he turned nasty.

The remaining questions related to my first visit to Seville, my journey to Malaga, etc. I had no desire to go into the personal psychological reasons that had moved me to stay in Malaga. I said that Miss Helena had already taken a note of all that.

In everything I said I kept to the truth, except on one point: to the question as to where I had obtained the material for my first book on Spain, I alleged that the "League for the Rights of Man" and other liberal organizations friendly to the Government had placed the material at my disposal; I had then put my signature to this data, trusting in the good faith of those organizations. All this was a lie; had I told the truth it might have cost several people in rebel territory their heads.

He asked me what sort of people the "secret wire-pullers of the Red Propaganda" in England were.

I named a list of twenty-five to thirty names that appear on appeals and notices of public meetings, all university professors and titled people, from knights upwards. When I came to "Her Grace the Duchess of Athole" he had had enough.

At the conclusion of the examination he said:

"When you were in National territory the first time, you weren't arrested?"

"No," I said.

"Extraordinary," he said.

And so it ended.

I came away from the examination very satisfied. At the beginning I had been afraid; the stupidity of the examiner had restored my self-confidence.

I related the whole story to Carlos with great gusto. He was a bad audience and grew more jumpy every minute. At last he said that he couldn't understand how I could be so cheerful after having discovered that I was to be charged with "aiding the military rebellion"; and that it was "absolutely ghastly."

This, of course, was sufficient to damp my spirits thoroughly, and I sat down to write a hurried S O S to the Consul.

When the Consul had first come to see me we had settled on a danger signal; if I underlined the date it would mean "S O S."

I wrote a letter containing nothing of importance, and underlined the date.

Sunday, May 9th.

Carlos has fairly got the wind up me. He paces about the cell and I realize that he already looks upon me as a dead man. He treats me with an exaggerated respect and consideration that get on my nerves. I have always preferred a harsh nurse to a sympathetic one. Pity is the echo of one's own misery and increases that misery fourfold.

Monday, May 10th.

The Consul came. He, too, appeared to be somewhat disquieted by the fact that I had been brought up for examination. It had still been impossible to obtain from Franco an assurance that he would not have me shot. He said, it is true, that he did not think my death was of such importance to Franco that he would risk offending the Foreign Office, but this was somewhat vague comfort. I asked if there were no possibility of my being exchanged with a prisoner of the Valencia Government, but he said that at the present stage he did not think it likely.

During our conversation I noticed that at short intervals I kept feeling dizzy and was unable to remember what had just been said. After fifteen days of fasting this was probably not to be wondered at. But I must have made an odd impression on him, and it seemed to me that he looked at me several times in astonishment and some irritation.

As a result, and after long weighing of the pros and cons, I have decided to start eating again. The main thing now is to keep a clear head at my trial.

And if this proves of no use, at least to cut a good figure.

Tuesday, May 11th.

Astonishing how quickly one picks up strength by eating again.

Was in the patio to-day for the first time for a week. The two Spaniards were horrified at my appearance. They had heard from Carlos yesterday that my trial was approaching and they hailed me with simulated heartiness. They said that it would be just the same with me as with them—I should be sentenced but not shot. Besides, they said, I had already been sentenced by court-martial and not shot, and that made me immune from a second sentence; it was like being inoculated against cholera.

All the time they were speaking I could not help thinking of how we had talked to Nicolás the day before he was executed.

I realize with surprise how comparatively safe I have been feeling all these last weeks. Now the button-counting will begin all over again, and the obsessive dance on the flagstones: if I tread in the middle, all will be well, but if I tread on the lines. . . .

There is nothing in the tenets of even the gloomiest monastic order which condemns a man to endure purgatory, and then, when it is all over, sends him back to hell.

Wednesday, May 12th.

Ten minutes ago I was told to pack my things, for I was going to be released.

I have put my toothbrush in my pocket.

Carlos is out in the patio. . . .

XX

THIS is a story without a climax.

For days on end we waited for the fall of Malaga as for the last act of a tragedy—and when Malaga fell we were not aware of it.

During the two months of my solitary confinement in Seville, I watched the football players in the courtyard—and did not know that at night they were shot.

Twice, for a total period of twenty-six days, I tormented myself with hunger and thirst; the object I wished to attain was each time rendered pointless by a strange freak of circumstance—and those against whom I waged this silent battle were not even aware of it.

Death tripped down the corridor, changing step, struck out here and there, danced pirouettes; often I felt his breath on my face when he was miles away; often I fell asleep and dreamed while he stood leaning over my bed.

This is a confused story without a definite thread, without climax or anti-climax. The corpses are not, as is fitting, piled up at the end of the act; they lie about, unevenly distributed, here, there and everywhere.

Often I wake at nights and think I am still in No. 41 and that it is not the Thames, at Shepperton, Middlesex, that runs past my window but the white taboo line in the great, dark patio.

Still more often I dream that I must return to No. 41 because I have left something behind there. I think I know what this something is, but it would be too complicated to explain.

The notes of the last post in the courtyard still ring in my ears.

Soon it will be night and evening has scarcely begun. In this country darkness falls the moment the sun has gone; there is no such word as "evening" in her language. The short span of twilight, which replaces evening, is not, as it is here, a gentle dying away of the day, but the beginning of night.

In this brief span, while the shadows swiftly glide along the walls and fill the patio with darkness, the last post is sounded.

Whilst the bugler sounds it, all is still in the courtyard. The prisoners stand to attention in a square. The sharp lines which suffering has seared into their faces are softened by the twilight. They listen to the bugler's notes, many of them open-mouthed; it is the only music they ever hear.

The bugler's last note goes on vibrating for a while. Until it has completely died away, the line of men stands to attention. The warder listens with head thrust forward to hear whether the last thin lingering note has ceased; then he blows his whistle.

The square turns right about; a second whistle, and it closes up and forms fours. Five minutes later the patio is dark and deserted.

Sometimes cats howl. When it is wet, the stars are reflected in the puddles. At full moon walls and gravel are a chalky white, and the cell windows yawn like black holes, emitting snores and groans.

There is a curious mechanism at work within us which romanticizes the past; the film of past experiences is coloured by the memory. It is a very primitive process, and the colours run into one another; maybe that is why they are so fairy-like. Often when I wake at night I am homesick for my cell in the death-house in Seville and, strangely enough, I feel that I have never been so *free* as I was then.

This is a very strange feeling indeed. We lived an unusual life on that patio; the constant nearness of death weighed down and at the same time lightened our existence. Most of us were not afraid of death, only of the act of dying; and there were times when we overcame even this fear. At such moments we were *free*—men without shadows, dismissed from the ranks of the mortal; it was the most complete experience of freedom that can be granted a man.

Such moments do not repeat themselves, and when one is back on the treadmill again all that remains is the feeling that one has forgotten something in Cell No. 41.

Those Militiamen in the great patio were amateurs in the art of warfare. They had been at the front, and yet they believed in miracles. Every day fresh news of victory went the rounds; to-day Toledo had been won back, next day Córdoba or Vitoria.

I was never able to discover the source of these rumours. They made the rounds of the prison, they were dropped in notes out of windows, they were whispered in the corridors. Was there someone in the building who purposely invented these stories of victory? Did those who passed them on believe in them, or did they only behave as if they believed?

Children sometimes stand before a mirror and make faces to frighten themselves. These prisoners did the opposite. They were niggardly of their feelings for each other, without sentimentality, sometimes without pity. But they fed each other's hopes because they could not bear to die without hope in a lost cause. To-day Toledo fell, the next day Burgos and Seville; they lied themselves to death as children cry themselves to sleep.

Only on one point was their information exact. Each of the thirteen hundred men in the prison knew how many had been shot the night before.

The criminals in the "beautiful patio" were nearly all of them bad cases. They resembled one another to an astonishing degree, although their heads were not all shaven and although they wore no uniform. They resembled each other just as old married couples resemble each other and old butlers resemble their masters.

I was only a quarter of a year in prison, but this period sufficed to give me some idea of the force of this process of protective coloration. From the very first day I felt that my new situation demanded of me a certain attitude, and the first time the warder put the broom into my hands I assumed without conscious reflection an air of distinguished incompetence, although during long years of bachelordom I had acquired a considerable degree of skill in the handling of a broom. The rôle I had to play in this building—the rôle of an innocent abroad—came to me automatically, and gradually, during the following weeks and months, became a mask, which did not require any conscious effort on my part. I was able to observe in a living example what direct biological force this process of protective coloration exerts.

Guilty or innocent, the prisoner changes form and colour, and assumes the mould that most easily enables him to secure a maximum of those minimal advantages possible within the framework of the prison system. In the world outside, now faded to a dream, the struggle is waged for position, prestige, power, women. For the prisoner those are the heroic battles of Olympian demi-gods. Here inside the prison walls the struggle is waged for a cigarette, for permission to exercise in the courtyard, for the possession of a pencil. It is a struggle for minimal and unworthy objects, but a struggle for existence like any other. With this difference, that the prisoner has only one weapon left to him: cunning and hypocrisy developed to the point of reflex action. Of all other means he has been deprived. The hearing and sense of touch of a man who has been blinded are intensified; there is only one direction in which the prisoner can evolve—that of increasing artfulness. In the hot-house atmosphere of his social environment he cannot escape this fateful transformation of his character. He feels his claws growing, a furtive and dejected, an impudent and servile look creeps into his eyes. His lips become thin, sharp, Jesuitical, his nose pinched and sharp, his nostrils dilated and bloodless; his knees sag, his arms grow long, and dangle gorilla-like. Those who uphold the Theory of Race and deny the influence of environment on the development of the human being should spend a year in prison and observe themselves daily in a mirror.

Long before I got to know Spain, I used to think of Death as a Spaniard. As one of those noble Señors painted by Velasquez, with black silk knee-breeches, Spanish ruff, and a cool, courteously indifferent gaze. He must have been pretty disgusted when they shot the unshaven Nicolás; indignant, he covered the little Militiaman's face with that mask of rigid dignity which is proper to the etiquette of his court.

There were thirteen hundred of us, his courtiers, in the Seville house of death. No liveried lackeys announced the approach of the noble Señor; the office of herald was performed by a greasy little priest, and the introduction of novices was carried out in a subdued whisper.

I came face to face with him once or twice. He only offered me his finger-tips; "How do you do?" he murmured. "See you later," and passed on, followed by the priest waving the sanctus bell.

He forgot his promise and did not come back; but *I* could not forget it, and I thought of it the whole time—it is always thus when one associates with the great.

There were thirteen hundred of us courtiers of the great Señor. We behaved boorishly. The simple peasants, in particular, those *pobres y humildes* with their uncouth manners, did not cut a good figure in the thin, tenuous air of the court. They appeared with full stomachs before the Señor, they stuffed themselves beforehand with beans; when they stood before his cool, bored countenance, they screamed with terror and called for help and for their mothers. They did not comply with the court etiquette, they asked foolish questions as to the Why and the Wherefore, they even forgot themselves so far as to call the black, greasy fellow with his bell a clown. Some of them sang the songs of the people; they sang them out of tune, in hoarse voices, and since they wept between-whiles, it sounded like belching. Even when the audience was over and the conventional rigid masks had been fitted on their faces, they did not make a good impression.

Nor did the atmosphere suit the others. The court librarian assumed grotesque bureaucratic manners; the officer evinced a most irregular sentimentality towards the Red mob; the man of facts became a moralist; the two friends who had been waiting together for months for their audience picked a quarrel in the very ante-chamber of the Señor. All averted their heads when someone else was writhing in agony; the fool they contemned and the dying they shunned.

The man with the sanctus bell, unworthy descendant of great ancestors, prattled of an ordeal that lay before all of us. We failed in this ordeal, but it was not our fault.

We all asked ourselves, whilst we waited, trembling, for the audience, to whose advantage and renown it was that we should be kept thus on the rack; what palpable or secret meaning there was behind it all? The peasants asked themselves in their way, the officer in his way, the man of facts in his. We plagued our brains with this question until the grey substance became inflamed and sweated forth blood and tears. Not one of us knew the answer, and least of all the man who rang the bell, the Señor's greasy major-domo.

XXI

Between the siesta and the evening meal the cell door flew open and freedom was hurled at me like a club; I was stunned, and stumbled back into life just as, had things taken another course, I should have stumbled into death.

As I stood in the corridor I shook from head to foot, overpowered by the same nervous trembling as on that night when someone outside my cell had called for help.

All that happened in the next few moments is dim in my memory, the contours blurred as though seen through a dense fog.

On the Governor's desk burns a naked electric bulb. All round it quivers an aura of light, like that through which one sees a street lamp flickering in a fog. In the Governor's chair sits a stranger. He is wearing a black shirt, without a tie. He bows with exaggerated formality.

"Señor," the man in the black shirt says, "I am taking you away from here." Again I have to hold on to the table; I feel dizzy and feverish; eating heartily after the long period of fasting has thoroughly upset my system.

"Señor," says the man in the black shirt, "I cannot tell you where I am taking you, but don't be afraid, we are *caballeros*."

We go along the lighted corridor, I don't know what is being done with me, I walk in my sleep. We go back to my cell, I shake Carlos by the hand, he is as thunderstruck as I; the door falls to between us before we can say a word to each other. Again we walk along the corridor; the loose leaves of my diary drop out of my pocket. The man in the black shirt helps me to pick them up. "What have you got there, Señor?" On the top is my wife's letter stamped by the censor. "Private letters," I murmur. "You can keep them, Señor, we are *caba-lleros.*" We go on down the corridor, open another cell door, I shake Byron and the consumptive by the hand; they are both frightened. "Where are they taking you?" "I don't know," I say, "God bless you," and the door falls to. We go on down the corridor and I shake hands—with Angel, Manuel the cripple, Don Ramón, Don Antonio.

Then we are back in the office.

"Señor," says the man in the black shirt, "we are now going to another town, and if you are prepared to promise certain things I may then be able to take certain steps to procure your release."

And he reaches out for pen and ink. When I see pen and ink, I wake up at once.

"My dear Sir," I say. "All this is so strange and so sudden. Who are you? What is this town you are taking me to? And what are these promises I am to make?"

"I would rather, Señor, not tell you my name. But we are *caballeros;* you can rely on us. We merely want you to promise that you will no longer meddle in the internal affairs of Spain. If you promise this, I may then be able to take certain steps to procure your release."

"I have never meddled in the internal affairs of Spain."

"You have engaged in a perfidious campaign against National Spain, Señor."

"I wrote what I saw and what I thought about it. I have never meddled in the internal affairs of Spain."

"I do not wish to argue with you, Señor. If you sign an undertaking that you will not meddle in the internal affairs of Spain I may then be able to take certain steps to procure your release. But we are not going to force you, we are *caballeros.*"

I signed a declaration to the effect that I had no intention of meddling in the internal affairs of Spain. I wrote further that I had been treated correctly in the prison of Seville.

I learned later that my release was neither an act of mercy nor a political gesture on the part of Franco. I was being exchanged with a prisoner of the Valencia Government. I learnt further details. The prisoner with whom I was exchanged was a certain Señora Haya, who was being held as a hostage in Valencia. The *caballero* in the black shirt was her husband, and one of Franco's most famous war pilots.*

Again we walked along the corridor, the man in the black shirt and I. A grille was pushed back, a key turned in the lock, a catch sprang back. Outside was the street.

Cars and donkey-carts were driving along the street. The people on the pavement walked here, there and everywhere in disorder, and not four abreast. A man leaned against the wall reading a newspaper. A child sat in the dust eating grapes.

In the garden outside the prison gate the guards stood about flirting with young girls. Girls with black hair; with roses stuck behind their ears, just as in Carmen. They wore skirts. They were quite wonderful girls.

"Señor," said the man in the black shirt. "If you have no objection, we will get into this car."

We got into the car. At the back sat two discreet detectives. One plunged his hand into his pocket; I thought he was going to bring out handcuffs, but it was a silver cigarette case.

We drove across the Guadalquivir; on the Guadalquivir there were ships. They trailed smoke behind them like loosened pigtails. They flew many-coloured flags. One blew its siren.

"Where are we going?" I asked.

"To another town," answered the man in the black shirt.

On the café terraces sat people reading newspapers and drinking coloured drinks. There was a deafening noise in the streets. We almost ran into a tram. Then we drove along an

---

* The *caballero* had been lying when he had said he "might be able to take steps to procure my release." The agreement with regard to the exchange had been signed twenty-four hours before, through the mediation of the British authorities.

avenue and the town was left behind. We drew up in an empty field and alighted. The *caballero* and the two detectives stood about irresolutely. For one last time the thought went through my mind: now they're going to draw their revolvers and shoot me down; then I heard the humming of an engine and a small open monoplane appeared from behind the bushes and came rolling along towards us.

A mechanic jumped out and saluted. The man in the black shirt climbed into the pilot's seat; the mechanic helped me to get in beside him; the detectives each took a wing and pushed.

We rolled along right across the field; behind the bushes lay the aerodrome. A whole herd of steel saurians was grazing there with outspread wings.

The *caballero* took the joy-stick; the earth tipped over obliquely and sank into the depths at our feet.

We were in an improbably small machine, an open Baby Douglas, as delicate as a child's toy. We rose higher and higher, the horizon expanded, the city of Seville shrank. The *caballero* in the black shirt pursed his lips—I heard nothing, but could tell that he was whistling a tune to himself.

"Where are we going, Señor?" I yelled.

"To another town, Señor," he yelled back.

We rose higher and higher. A mountain loomed towards us. White shreds of mist floated round us on all sides. The *caballero* in the black shirt pointed to the abyss below.

"All this is National Spain, Señor," he yelled. "Here everyone is happy now."

"What?" I yelled.

". . . happy," he yelled, "happy and free."

"What?" I yelled.

"Free."

We were silent, and only the engine thundered. The shreds of mist below us fused into a white plateau; the earth was no longer to be seen. The *caballero* sat with legs apart, the joy-stick between his knees, and gesticulated with his hands. "On your side the poor fight against the rich. We have a new system. We do not ask whether a man is rich or poor, but whether he is good or bad. The good poor and the good rich are on one side. The bad poor and the bad rich on the other. That is the truth about Spain, Señor."

"How do you distinguish them?" I asked.

"What?" he yelled.

"How do you distinguish them?"

We soared again; by now we must be right over the mountains. The engine thundered, for a while I could hear nothing.

"In their hearts all Spaniards are on our side," screamed the *caballero* in the black shirt. "When the Reds shoot our people, their last cry is our cry of '*Viva España*.' I have seen several Reds being shot, and they too cried at the end '*Viva España*.' In the hour of death men speak the truth. You will see from this that I am right, Señor."

"Did you look?" I yelled.

"What?" he yelled back.

"I asked whether you looked while they were shot."

We hovered above the white plateau; we saw nothing but the white plateau below us and felt as though we were hovering over one spot. The *caballero* sat with his legs apart and gesticulated with his hands; the engine worked by itself. We had no need to do anything, we simply sat there on a hovering raft above the clouds and looked down.

"When one sits here like this," yelled the man in the black shirt, "one thinks a good deal about life and death. The Reds are all cowards; they don't even know how to die. Can you imagine what it is like to be dead?"

"Before we were born, we were all dead," I yelled.

"What?" he yelled.

"I say before we were born we were all dead."

"That is true," he yelled. "But why, then, is one afraid of death?"

"I have never been afraid of death, but only afraid of dying," I yelled.

"With me it's exactly the opposite," yelled the man in the black shirt.

Rifts appeared in the white plateau below us. A gust of wind struck us, the 'plane trembled and began to gambol like a colt. The *caballero's* hands were once more occupied, and he was silent.

I felt feverish again. If the *caballero* were to make a false movement now, the earth would rush up at us and strike us dead. That would be a fine end, I thought, with an almost mythological touch about it. Death has no terrors, only dying —must that not be the same with everyone? But the *caballero* maintains that with him it is the opposite. The *caballero* is a damned clever pilot; presumably he is also a damned fine bomb-thrower. Carlos too is an officer, and he too is not afraid of dying. But the thought of death paralysed his legs and left him as helpless as a child that has not yet learned to walk.

Carlos and the *caballero* both know how to die; they are officers; dying is their *métier*. It has been drilled into them, it is in their bones: to die with an air.

Little Nicolás certainly did not die with an air. He was a civilian. The Militiamen in the patio were civilians too. They had no experience of dying. They were terribly afraid of dying. Up above the clouds circled the *caballero* and hurled bombs down on them with an air; they threw themselves on their stomachs and grovelled in the mud and were afraid. Often, when the machine-guns began to bark, they did the natural thing and ran away; before they were shot they called for help and for their mothers. They liked playing football, nibbling lettuce and dreaming of the time after the war when they would all learn to read. And when they would be no more than three in a room, and be able to eat meat twice a week, and buy themselves a Sunday suit and a watch, for when the war was over, life would really begin. They believed that it was good and necessary to live, and even to fight in order to live, and even to die so that others might live. They believed in all this, and because they believed truly in it, because their lives depended on this belief, they were not afraid of death. But they were terribly afraid of dying. For they were civilians, soldiers of the people, soldiers of life and not of death.

I was there when they died. They died in tears, crying vainly for help, and in great weakness, as men must die. For dying is a confoundedly serious thing, one shouldn't make a melodrama of it. Pilate did not say *"Ecce heros"*; he said *"Ecce homo."*

We were hovering again. The *caballero* in the black shirt waved his arms afresh and yelled out metaphysical catchwords that were as insubstantial as the mist below us and caused as much palpable mischief as the bombs that he hurls below. I would gladly have thrown him out of the 'plane, but he was at the controls, and he was stronger than I.

EPILOGUE

THE town to which the *caballero* in the black shirt had brought me was La Linea, the Spanish frontier town adjoining Gibraltar.

I had to wait forty-eight hours in the La Linea prison. On May 14th I trod British soil as a free man.

A week later the consumptive was put to death by the *vile garotte*. For certain reasons the time has not yet come to publish his name. Byron was sentenced to thirty years' hard labour.

The *caballero* met his death in an air battle over Teruel in the spring of 1938.

Those who survived are now pursuing their dialogues with death in the midst of the European Apocalypse, to which Spain had been the prelude.